Dreams...Promises...A Vanner Horse Journey

Dreams... Promises...

A Vanner Horse Journey

JOYCE M. CHRISTIAN

COVER PHOTO BY VANESSA WRIGHT CAPONE

iUniverse, Inc.
Bloomington

Dreams...Promises...A Vanner Horse Journey

iUniverse books may be ordered through booksellers or by contacting:

iUniverse
1663 Liberty Drive
Bloomington, IN 47403
www.iuniverse.com
1-800-Authors (1-800-288-4677)

ISBN: 978-1-4502-8639-8 (sc)
ISBN: 978-1-4502-8427-1 (ebk)

Printed in the United States of America

iUniverse rev. date: 01/25/2011

Dedication

My first attempt at telling my story was dedicated completely to Cindy Thompson, who was totally captivated by this horse and had the wisdom to see its gifts for humankind. As time passed without publishing my work, my story grew and so did those who deserve to be thanked for their support and friendship along the way.

Therefore, I begin this dedication again......dedicating this work now to not only Cindy, but to Cushti Bok, the little stallion that generated the first spark of curiosity within her; that opened the door for the Thompsons to uncover his heritage and in so doing finding the beginnings of a new breed. To Dennis Thompson without whose passion, and ability to see the potential of these horses, they might have been lost.

This finished work is a reality because of the support, encouragement, and honest to goodness friendship required to get me through it all. These needed ingredients were provided generously by these very close friends at critical times during the journey: Kathy Sommers, Allyson Pritchard, Deb Menkens, Dianna Guldjberg, Linda Sibilia, Paula and Deanna Lynch, Darla and Dana Monte, and Carliss Henderson.

I want to thank my daughters. Jamie for being a constant in listening, encouraging, and making me laugh when I did not think I could. Jill for coming home time and time again; for making it real, for being a vital part of what this has always been about – a home with

1

the horses – and for bringing with her, Aidan, who simply makes it all the more richer.

Finally, but certainly not the least, it is dedicated to my horse, Bandit, whose beauty and incredible differences set him apart from other horses and made me wonder, question, and desire to know why.

Joyce M. Christian

Cindy Thompson with Cushti Bok the first day they met.
(Photo courtesy of Dennis Thompson)

"Whatever you hope or dream of achieving, regardless of what area of your life it pertains to, you are not going to stumble into it. Dream, Plan, Execute."

- Matthew Kelly, author of The Dream Manager

oday my retirement became a reality. I met with Blue Cross Blue Shield representative, Ruth White, to discuss my health insurance policy and any changes to expect upon retirement. Ruth has been a joy to do business with over my time here in New York. She remembers that personal connection that endears her to each of her clients. Without fail, as I pushed my chair from the conference table, she began, "So, how are those ponies of yours?" Such a question, she knows, goes straight to my heart and of course will keep me at the table for at least another fifteen minutes. As I shared my latest excitement I noticed tears well up in her eyes. She smiled and said, "You have a gift for storytelling, you need to share this in a book.

Well, this book has been a work in progress for the last ten years. Ruth's words of encouragement sent me back to the computer with a new energy to tell this story. I have struggled for some time with how to begin it. I have wadded up all the other efforts and begin anew here with my favorite opening to any tale.......

Once upon a time......

...there was a little girl growing up in rural Alabama in the 1950's. She watched "Gunsmoke" every Saturday night with her father over at Mr. Sid and Miss Maggie's house. They were the first ones in the area to get a television. Then of course it didn't take long for her father to bite the bullet and buy a set as well.

The addiction to TV Westerns grew. She fell in love, not with Gene Autry or Roy Rogers, but with Champion and Trigger. One branch on the beautiful cedar tree in the front yard was permanently bent from the child pretending to ride a horse for hours.

Later her family moved to the small farm up the road. There the path along the edge of the woods was worn bare from the thousand imaginary rides on a stick horse. This house had a front porch. Each Christmas from 1955 to 1960 found a rope tied securely to the porch post. The plea for Santa to bring a real pony was always number one on the wish list. Annually on Christmas morning the rope was found lying lifeless where it had been left with so much hope. Yet, the girl continued to dream – she loved horses – why she did not know, she just knew that she did.

Divorce came and brought changes the girl would accept in time. She and her sister and mother moved to town to live with her aging great aunt. No farm, no woods, just a busy street in front of the house. Yet, here in town friends with horses would share, and hours of pleasure and fun would be enjoyed. One such friend owned a frisky and sometimes willing pony named Darby. In a neighbor's large open field the children would all take turns riding. Sometimes as single riders and the smaller kids would often double up. Darby appeared to enjoy those afternoons as much as his young riders.

However, he had a way to let them know when it was time to quit. There was a Mimosa tree with a low hanging branch. It was at exactly the right height to knock off an unsuspecting rider should Darby go in that direction. The children's laughter and Darby's whinny of delight could be heard throughout the neighborhood on those charmed afternoons.

Even into her high school years she treasured those memories. Now more demanding school work and part time jobs would fill her days, yet the warm Alabama summers would bring the promise of the annual horse show. An event she had learned to anticipate with great pleasure. Her earliest recollection of the horse show was when she was six years old. Her parents had taken her. A man had a "live carousel". The ponies were all hitched to this contraption and walked in endless circles providing the many children maybe their first and only ride on a horse. Of course, the girl took such a ride and when it ended she refused to get off the pony to her mother's dismay.

After much begging the kindhearted man gave her a free ride. A photo was taken and remains to this day a favorite reminder of this special childhood moment.

Riding and dreaming on the Pony Ride at the Fairgrounds where the Annual Horse Show was held. (1957)

As the girl grew older her eagerness to attend the horse show only increased, something her mother could not understand. Still she more often than not drove her daughter to the fairgrounds, dropped her off and scheduled a pick up time, which of course for the girl was always too early. No matter, time there would be spent watching beautiful horses from all over the state compete in a variety of disciplines. She could only imagine what it must feel like to own such beautiful creatures. Every horse sleek, shiny and groomed to perfection; riders dressed in their finest only added to their horse's beauty and performance. The girl sat mesmerized event after event, day after day, summer after summer. This annual experience fueled the dream that one day she would have a horse of her own.

Another summer pleasure was more time to read. The girl loved books and the town library was only blocks from her house. Her mother gladly gave permission for her to spend hours there. When she closes her eyes even now she can still hear the familiar creak to the library door and the instant delightful smell of the books awaiting her. She knew the shelves that housed the Walter Farley, *Black Stallion* books, as well as *Misty of Chincoteague* and of course Anna Sewell's beloved *Black Beauty* like she knew the back of her hand. If those library cards were still around today they would declare who loved those books best – the girl's name was repeated over and over as she checked out these favorites and read them multiple times. Even when other sixteen year olds were delving into young romance stories and other teenage interests she returned once again to her horse books with an insatiable appetite.

I am that girl. My lifetime pursuit of my childhood dream became a reality in the Spring of 1997 when at the age of forty-six I became a horse owner for the very first time. The story of that purchase and the journey it began fills the remaining pages of this book.

The Miriam-Webster Online Thesaurus provides
the following for the word – "magical":
Entry Word:
magical
Function:
adjective
Text: 1. being or appearing to be under a magic spell:
ENCHANTED *2. being so extraordinary or abnormal as to suggest*
powers which violate the laws of nature; SUPERNATURAL
3. having seemingly supernatural qualities or powers.

I looked this up as I don't want to wear out the word throughout my story, however after carefully reading the meaning provided, there have been moments in the last thirty years I fear cannot be explained without its use. The first occurred in March of 1978. On a whim, and because we were young and adventurous my friend, Kathy Noland and I, both elementary school teachers applied to teach overseas with the Department of Defense Schools. We barely got our applications in by the cutoff in January. Kathy received a letter indicating she had been selected for an interview to be held in Atlanta, Georgia in March. We hopefully anticipated such a message for me. It never came.

We accepted that Kathy would go to Europe and I would visit. However, that was not good enough for one of the educational aides at Vance Elementary School where we worked. She knew one of the Alabama Senators personally and felt I deserved an interview. As I was going about my daily routine of teaching a reading group I was interrupted and summoned to the main office where I was told the Senator was on the phone for me.

He greeted me as if we had known each other forever and apologized that such an oversight had occurred. He told me his secretary had spoken with the individual in Washington who set up the interviews and I would be receiving a phone call that evening to schedule mine.

As promised the phone rang and a pleasant woman's voice wanted to know what date and time would work best for my interview. I gave her Kathy's appointment date hoping we could travel together. Total astonishment flooded Kathy's face as she heard me thank the woman not only for the same date but the time slot prior to her own.

The day arrived. I was invited into a small cubicle. The interviewer looked at me with a penetrating sort of stare and began, "What makes you so different?" Before I could even pull my thoughts together he continued, "Do you see that stack of folders?" "Yes", I replied. His voice took on a fatherly tone as he shared that all the candidates in the stack wanted the chance to work overseas. Unfortunately he would be forced to consider me ahead of them. The puzzled look on my face must have been what made him turn over the folder, lying all by itself, next to the fifty folder stack. My eyes rested on the bold red large print that ran from the bottom left corner to the top right corner of the folder, "CONGRESSIONAL APPOINTEE".

My expression and tone must have given him cause to reconsider my situation. I quickly began rambling on about the Senator's phone call and how I had not asked for help. Almost at the point of tears I told him I was so sorry and would be willing to simply remove my application and have my friend join him for her legitimate interview.

A smile creased his mouth and he started, "Well, let's see how you do with the questions." He began with a typical battery, none of which I remember now. However, it is impossible for me to forget him asking me if I would accept ANY assignment that might be offered. He really didn't want me to be like the majority of those other congressional appointees, whose uncle or relative got them the job; then once onsite they didn't like the climate, or the language was too difficult, or the lack of familiar comforts found them returning to the USA – costing the government thousands. I can still see his animated face and hear his voice as he asked, "What if they offer you, Bahrain? Do you know they have spiders there t-h-i-s big?" Both of his ample arms were stretched as far apart as space would allow, as he continued, "What would you do?"

It was here that I decided I had done nothing wrong and it was time to fight for this opportunity. I leaned forward looked him straight in the eye and replied, "I'd find a really b-i-g stick."

"I believe you would", I heard him saying as he stood, thanking me for my time and informing me that I would hear within the next two months if I was selected for a position. He opened the door; I thanked him and he invited Kathy to come in.

In August of 1978 Kathy and I found ourselves on a plane headed to Frankfurt, Germany. Amazingly we had both been assigned to a new

American school located in Osterholz-Scharmbeck, Germany. And so began my first of twenty-three years in Europe.

For someone who looks for and enjoys fantasy in her life, it seemed rather appropriate that my first apartment in Germany would be located only a few miles from Bremen. Yes, home of the "Bremen Town Musicians" and indeed a statue stands just off the town square dedicated to this wonderful tale. The village in which I lived had its own charm. Worpswede is located on the river Hamme northeast of Bremen in the Teufelsmoor (devil's bog). Home to what would become known as the Worpswede Artist Colony. It is a wealth of art history, museums, and picturesque landscapes that I have not found anywhere else in my travels. A favorite print of an Otto Modersohn painting is always hung wherever I call home. It is a beautiful scene of the moon over the Teufelsmoor. Whenever I look at it I cannot help but smile and remember the wonderful experience of living in that little village and learning so much about Germany and its people. I lived in Worpswede for five years.

I left Germany briefly in 1983 and returned home to Alabama to give birth to my first daughter. She and I returned to Germany in the summer of 1984 and began our lives in the Frankfurt area. Though the hustle and bustle of city life was only a short drive from us we found our greatest pleasure in a three hundred year old farm house that had been beautifully renovated. It was located in the farming village of Niedermittlau and owned by an elderly couple, Erich and Maria Schmitt. Erich was a language teacher speaking English, French, Spanish and of course German fluently. A second daughter was born here and the Schmitt's became Oma and Opa to my children.

Erich would require me to speak German, which I will forever be indebted to him for making me accomplish. Though I am in no way fluent I can understand and carry a conversation in the country I dearly love as my second home. It was here that my farm roots would be awakened and I began to want the childhood experiences that were so important to me for my girls.

Our house was nestled at the foot of Bear's Head Mountain, so named because of its shape. If you looked closely you could really see the bear's head. If you walked from our house towards the mountain you came to a small farm. The farmer kept chickens, ducks and a goat named Heidi.

My girls were introduced early on to this menagerie. We fed the chickens and ducks that ran and quickly waddled to get the tasty bread crumbs. These walks, bicycle rides, afternoons at the playground, and tea under the cherry tree in our backyard remain precious memories for all of us. We spent twelve years in the unhurried world of Niedermittlau while I taught first at Gelnhausen American Elementary School and then later at Argonner Elementary School located in Hanau; home to none other than the Brothers Grimm.

Down came the Berlin Wall, the Cold War dissipated and the American Force reduction in Europe began. With this downsizing the need for American military schools decreased significantly causing personnel to be reassigned throughout Europe and the Pacific. With these changes a new school for me was not a choice but a reality. It was 1995 and we found ourselves moving to Bitburg.

Change is never an easy thing. Uprooting two girls at the beginning of the second decade of their lives only added to my sadness of having to relocate. Of course first on the "To Do" list was to find a house or an apartment. A friend knew of a family PCSing, military lingo for Permanent Change of Station. The house would soon be available and I scheduled an appointment to see it. As I drove through the gentle rolling hills from Bitburg to the village of Biersdorf a smile could not be contained – it was farm land, beautiful, working and well kept farms. The road wound its way amidst the hills like a ribbon looping through one village and then the next. Arriving in Biersdorf I found the street and made a left. At the end of a cul-de-sac was the house; modern and very American looking with a nice yard. Tall evergreens adorned the lawn and reminded me I was in Germany and not America. I rang the door bell.

I was greeted by the lady of the house and invited in. A quick glance even from the foyer let me know this would be a great home. A brick fireplace in one corner of the spacious open living area would be welcomed on cold, snowy winter evenings. The best selling point however was the number of bedrooms promising each daughter a room of her own!

In less than a month my daughters and I along with our West Highland Terrier, MacIntosh, had arrived and unpacked in the Biersdorf house. It was a difficult move; the first in their lives for my daughters. My oldest took less time to settle in while my youngest just starting Middle School struggled and missed her Oma and Opa terribly. Being a single parent and having the sole responsibility for raising my girls seemed harder in this new place.

I too missed Erich and Maria and their support and encouragement. It was a lonely beginning. I found myself looking forward to walking the dog. The farmers' access roads to the fields ran beside and behind our house. These were perfect for walking with Mac and gave me time to think, pray, and hope for the best. On these walks I began to see horses in paddocks down below. I had noticed a sign for a riding school at the bottom of our hill.

Jill recalls it was her friend, Colleen, who encouraged her to take riding lessons. I simply remember one day driving home she asked about riding. I could not have been happier! She would take the bus home; do homework and walk down to the stables. I would stop on my way home and see what was happening. Some days I'd see a lesson in progress, other days I didn't see her, but knew she was with the girls and horses in the barn. This was reassuring. I felt comfortable knowing she was safe and enjoying this new found interest.

One evening Jill came home from her riding lesson all excited. Rudy, her instructor had invited us to attend a horse show on Sunday. My mind did a flashback to Alabama summers and horse shows of so long ago. Not even in my wildest imagination could I have prepared myself for what was about to happen in my life.

On that fateful Sunday afternoon, Jill and I arrived at the riding arena. The front of which had been prepared for an audience. Tables and chairs were arranged for best viewing and we found one at the front. Rudy welcomed his visitors and then it happened........one of those life altering moments. The back door of the arena opened and a young girl mounted on the most magical horse I had ever seen entered. I blinked my eyes like you do when you think the light is playing tricks on you. It didn't seem quite real at first, but it was. Hair was everywhere; long, flowing mane and tail that either touched the ground or met the feathers covering the hooves. He was magnificent! Brown and white, mostly white, average sized, but appeared strong, powerful, with the gentleness you want in a family's pet. His movement was enchanting; he appeared to float as he moved around the ring. As I was about to convince myself of his reality, I was once again swept away to another realm as four others equally as beautiful joined him in the ring. There was nothing else to do but to simply enjoy, take it all in, admire and certainly begin to question why I had never seen such horses before.

I did not want this to end. Yet, I needed answers to the questions that were rapidly growing in my mind and stretching my imagination. I glimpsed a smile of understanding on Rudy's face.

He recognized my plight and there was a sense of playfulness in the twinkle I caught in his eye. He knew something, maybe a secret; he was sharing it by letting us see these wonderful horses, yet there was so much more he still had hidden. I wanted him to tell me everything!

When the show ended Jill escaped and went to the barn to meet her friends who had been the fortunate riders. I waited to speak with Rudy. He said they were gypsies' horses from England. I had been to England and seen gypsies travelling along the roadsides with their horses, yet never had I seen anything like these animals. Rudy read the interest on my face and continued, "....they are special horses from the gypsies." I had to agree, that they were.

13

Up until this day I had loved all horses equally. I had never really thought about having a favorite breed or color. I grew up dreaming of The Black Stallion, but some days Roy Rogers' palomino, Trigger, would have my heart. It was simple – I just loved horses – until today.

Monday after work I drove straight to the riding arena. Sleep had been difficult in coming the night before and throughout my work day my mind wandered back to that horse. To solve my problem I decided to return to the scene of the crime. Yes, crime – complete mental take over! As I approached the arena door I saw that the show horses were practicing. They were performing a variety of tricks. One horse was being encouraged to step up on a pedestal; while two others were learning to see-saw! I was intrigued. The beautiful Buck (the show horse) was being ridden back and forth through a curtain made out of strips of ripped tarp. It didn't bother him at all; he just trotted right through with confidence. There was a basket in the corner filled with day old rolls and bread. The girls would come by, stuff rolls in their pockets and when the horses did the trick they were immediately rewarded with the bread which they appeared to really enjoy.

Rudy who was standing mid arena suddenly noticed me. As he approached his smile revealed he was pleased I was back and more so that I had really been impressed with these horses. With his broken English and my broken German we were quite the pair, but communication was usually successful.

He and his brother, Herbert, ran the riding school. I gathered over time that his father had been a well respected equestrian and Rudy had followed in those footsteps. Photos adorned the walls of the visitors' viewing booth telling in their visual way the history of the Klaes family and their love of horses.

Now he stood by my side watching the girls as they finished their work and were beginning to lead the horses back to the barn. He began, "I have wanted to talk with you about Jill. She is very good and I want to move her from the beginning group to the intermediate group for lessons." I was so pleased that she was doing well and was enjoying the horses. I had hoped at least one of my daughters would be bitten by the bug. It obviously was going to be Jill as Jamie had shown no interest whatsoever.

Throughout the next couple of months Jill continued to progress and was eventually moved to the advanced group. Rudy would laugh and tell me she had Velcro butt. His only concern and mine as well was she simply showed no fear. She rode with vigor; jumped; cantered like the wind always with a smile stretching from ear to ear. Oh, and if anyone noticed the mom at the gate her smile mirrored that of her daughter. I could not have been more pleased, yes for Jill but also for me to have this opportunity to be around horses once again.

As time went by I found myself stopping by the stable and riding arena often. I would watch the classes and the practices with the special horses. Rudy had a variety of horses, old ones, young ones, many different types and breeds. The horses he had purchased from the British gypsies continued to capture my attention to the greatest degree. I truly wanted to understand why I had never seen them before and why when I questioned Rudy he seemed at a loss for answers as well.

Rudy's riding school was no different from a hundred others throughout Germany. Riding lessons were conducted year round. However, late spring, summers and into the fall were indeed busy times. People would arrive during these times for their equestrian vacations or in some cases just "country" escape from the busy cities. I learned that not all of the horses could be used for these individuals as many came with little or no horse experience. Weekly riding camps for horse crazy girls would fill before summer even arrived. Therefore, Rudy was always looking for horses to meet the needs of his guests. The horses from the gypsies were being used more and more and soon people were requesting them.

Rudy was making trips to England about every three months to find and purchase horses. The large barn at the rear of the riding school was labeled "the sale barn". Horses were moved there to be sold or those just coming in were sometimes housed there until it was determined if they would indeed be kept. I began to make frequent visits to this barn. I was somewhat baffled by the differences in a group of horses just arrived from England.

The five eating away at their hay could have cared less about me. Their coats were a bit straggly and manes and tails were broken or more than likely chewed off. I could tell the thickness might eventually return. They were either black and white or brown and white. This group certainly had a ways to go to come close to the amazing Buck, Gangster, and the others in the show group.

The warm spring days were returning. Though I thoroughly enjoyed German winters and taking my girls skiing in our favorite areas: Berchesgarten, Northern Italy, and Switzerland, the return of warmer days were always eagerly anticipated by this Alabama girl.

On such a day as I drove into the riding school courtyard Rudy motioned for me to join him at the outside table. As I relaxed into the chair I was saying how much I enjoyed "die Fruhling". He tolerated my German. As he began in English I knew how well I obviously was doing in mutilating his native tongue. He always began our conversations with praise for Jill and her natural ability. He had grown quite fond of her. By this time her favorite place was this riding school. She loved the girls who now were her best friends, and the horses who were their willing partners.

Today's conversation went in a different direction. He was talking to me about the horses. His tone was soft and I had to lean closer in order to hear. He was telling me that his neighbor, Herr Theisen was a very nice man and he had a barn. Then without any change of tone he delivered the punch line….."I think Jill needs a horse of her own and Herr Theisen could rent you a stall."

I was surprised, certainly not what I had ever considered or even thought about. We were living in Germany, why or better yet how could we have a horse? I wanted to continue our conversation about the horses hoping to learn answers to my questions that had greatly multiplied over time – not discuss buying one!

When my shock subsided Rudy's gaze was resting on me. A slight mischievous grin was curling the corners of his mouth. Before I could think further he continued, "I've spoken with Herr Theisen and he has a stall he will rent to you.....of course Jill could use the facilities here and continue her lessons, but now on a horse of her own."

I heard Jill and her friends coming through the courtyard archway. Rudy stood up and said I could think about his offer. He walked by the girls and was gone from my sight.

My mind did battle over the days that followed. I kept going from reality to the fulfillment of a childhood dream – to own a horse! How old was I, how long had I waited? This was not for me though, it would be for Jill. She truly had a gift and I needed to do this for her. To buy a horse would be right - for both of us, yes? I continued to question myself. The frugal, steady, no nonsense me was completely obliterated by the fanciful, hopeful dreamer.

The next thing I knew I was standing with Jill and Rudy looking at the latest arrivals from England. No need to look at any other kind of horse, we had to have a special horse from the gypsies and maybe then I could begin to answer those questions. A mare, black and white, with an intelligent eye had captured Jill's attention.

Rudy said she was a three year old. Her head was larger than I liked from studying the show horses, but her pattern was lovely and I liked her eyes. "Is this the one you want?" I heard my voice asking my daughter. She was already quietly stroking the mane away from the neck and I heard her whisper, "Yes."

Rudy and I walked back to his office where I finalized the purchase of our first horse. We then walked out into the sunshine and across the street where Herr Theisen stood in the cobblestoned farmyard. We were introduced and he showed us the front of the cow barn that had been converted into a couple of stalls for horses.

We discussed the rent and I explained my daughter and I would do all the work. He would supply hay and there would be adequate paddock space for turnout daily. Jill named the mare, Magic. She accepted the Theisen's barn as her home without complaint and so began our lives with horses.

Alfonz and Barbara Theisen welcomed us as family in no time at all. Of course, I soon learned the ulterior motive. The Theisens had a Shetland pony named, Moritz. Ah Moritz, he so reminded me of the Darby of long ago; just as obstinate and playful. Alfonz told Jill he would be happy for her to ride Moritz anytime she wished. In fact there was encouragement in this invitation. The Thiesens had two vacation cottages. Throughout the season families came with young children who wanted to "ride the pony". The only problem was Moritz had not been ridden or exercised enough and had grown quite fond of the lazy life. He wasn't really safe for visiting children. Then he met Jill.

Experience, up until now, had taught her she could ride any horse. Her "Velcro butt" had guaranteed her success. Now there was Moritz. He bucked; she hit the cobblestones, providing her first fall from a horse. Thank goodness it was only a short distance to the ground. She adored Moritz and he in turn was obviously thrilled to have "a girl of his own". We grew to love him as if he was ours.

Alfonz taught me much about barn care, German style. He used straw as bedding and hay was stored in large round bales. Cleaning stalls was not an everyday chore; sometimes not even an every week chore. It was the German farmer's way. He said the manure made soft, warm bedding under the straw. This I could not understand for spring months and I certainly did not intend to comply. Our Magic was a princess. Her stall was cleaned daily, either by Jill or me; maybe there were days when we both did it unbeknownst to the other. My weekends suddenly changed; no longer just walking the dog, a little school work followed by a video or a good book.

Now, I awoke on Saturday mornings eager to start my day. I could hardly wait to get to the barn. If Jill had Magic out with a group on the trails which was the routine, I not only cleaned her stall but tackled Moritz's as well. I loved every minute in the barn! I could not have been happier about all the work that came with it.

The girl in me wanted to just take Magic out of her stall, put her on the cross ties, brush her, and take her for a walk. Yet, it had been twenty years since I'd been around horses and my lack of confidence and adult need to be safe prohibited me from doing as I wished.

However, I was happy to be the observer as Magic and Jill formed a partnership. It was parental pride and my dream combined. As I watched I became aware of something other than whimsical beauty; an uncanny intelligence was evident in this mare. She learned quickly and soon she and Jill were riding in lessons, on trails, and at show practices.

All of Rudy's lesson horses showed their own smarts; even the mischievous Moritz. Yet, Magic's expressions appeared more meaningful; her eyes were soft and truly loving. Each day assured me that buying this horse had been right. Not just for Jill, not just for me, maybe for Magic as well.

This mare had indeed brought an element of enchantment; a return of childhood wonder and belief into my life. She provided a safe zone; a no worry place for my young daughter. While Jamie was drifting towards boys, the latest hair and nail color, this month's songs and jeans, Jill was discovering a natural talent with a forever friend. Saturday morning rides often included a stop by our house for a snack or drink. I recall one such Saturday.

I stood on our porch and Jill rode Magic at a full gallop back and forth in the field across the road – it was beautiful – the horse unlike any I had seen or known – white mane floating in the breeze earning her name – my daughter happy, care free, and confident.

19

**Magic stepping up on the front porch of our house
in Biersdorf, Germany**

At the end of the ride they crossed the street and into our yard; Jill dismounted and dropped the reins for Magic to graze while she grabbed a drink. Magic, surprisingly instead of grazing followed Jill and walked up on the porch as if she planned to come inside as well. I thought you smart, smart girl.

Finally the day came when my courage and desire collided and I decided I would try and ride Magic. Jill had warmed her up and I stepped onto the mounting block and into the saddle. Memories came flooding back; the feel, the smell, the fun! We started walking and I was so excited. Confident I decided to urge her into a trot.....well, she began a nice little trot and I began a nice little slip to the side. I was sliding, Magic continued trotting and I continued sliding, I saw the dirt of the arena floor and like in a slow motion moment knew I was going to meet it. However, just when I thought I was losing my hold suddenly, miraculously I was able to right myself. We finished the circle around the arena and with a real sense of success I dismounted. Jill and friends withheld their laughter though smiles were visible. It probably did look somewhat humorous to girls who rode effortlessly; this forty something woman holding on for dear life.

It was obvious my skills were twenty years rusty and I was certain they had never been as accomplished as my audience. No matter, my successful ride around the arena encouraged me to take a few, yes, beginning riding lessons. Those helped me to understand maybe at this late date riding wasn't going to be my strength.

While giggling girls brushed manes, tails and feathers in the courtyard, I often walked on through the barn and back to the sale barn. I would stop and spend a few minutes at each stall looking carefully at its occupant.

Frequent observations helped me to begin to identify the look and characteristics setting these horses from the gypsies apart. Soon I began to even categorize them into groups; the mediocre, the average, the ones like Buck! The last category was the anomaly. It was a strange world in which I found myself – living in Germany; owning a horse, different and unusual creating more questions for me than answers.

Now as I look back, it was very near perfect the little village of Biersdorf, nestled amongst low rolling hills. Farmers' fields and pastures with cows, sheep and where horses adorned the countryside. I can still smell the fresh produce in the markets; flowers in the spring their fragrance pungent and sweet. My mouth waters when I remember the *"backerei"* filled with *"brotchen"*, breads, and pastries unique to this country I had come to love. Now it held yet another claim to my affection, it had afforded me the opportunity to not only be with horses once again, but to own our Magic!

After a time I began to convince myself that buying another horse would be possible. Yes, I was slowly beginning to slip into insanity. I wanted one of my own. Not just any horse, and not just any gypsy horse – I wanted the anomaly – I wanted a Buck!

I told Rudy I had decided on a second horse. He was happy to hear this as he was in every sense of the word a salesman; a real horse trader. As I explained exactly what I was looking for his smile lessened and he said, "Horses like that are very hard to find. Even if I was lucky enough to find one, the gypsy wouldn't sell it." "Why is that?" I questioned. "You make trips to England; you buy horses from gypsies and bring them here. I agree most are not anything special, but occasionally there is one that makes even you excited. Most often you keep that one. I've been studying the ones like Buck, Rudy. They are like no other breed. Their build is their own; strong and bold, yet small and elegant; tons of hair, mane, tail, and feathers. Gentle, intelligent eyes look out from a head that is in no way drafty, it is perfect for each of them. The size of the head balances the body to which it is attached, finishing off the most beautiful look I have ever encountered. I want one of those." He walked away sadly shaking his head.

A few days later, on one of my routine strolls through the sale barn my eyes were adjusting to the light when I noticed a black horse in the stall in front of me. I walked closer blinking a couple of times to focus properly, he was beautiful! As I stood there trying to draw his attention away from his hay, Rudy walked in.

"I know what you're thinking. He isn't for sale. I'm keeping him a few days before taking him to his new owner in southern Germany. The lady is a friend of the gypsy's family", he shared. "I see", I said with a sigh. "I want one like him, Rudy, please." With understanding in his voice he said, "I know." It was clear he understood my disappointment. The black horse was gone the next time I went to visit. I was sad.

The three months of summer had lazily passed. I was working in my school office in preparation for the opening of school coming up faster than I liked when my phone rang. It was Jill. She was speaking quickly and excitedly as she shared, "Mom, the black horse is back!" She wanted me to leave immediately, as did I but had to finish my work day.

As soon as was possible I was out the door driving much faster than the Politzei would like I sped to the barn. My heart was racing as I entered; there in the back stall was the horse, the one who had so disappointed me by leaving. He seemed unaffected by me standing and watching while he stood eating. I found it hard to believe he was really back.

Rudy walked up behind me and as if he was reading my mind explained, "The lady wanted a trail horse. This is a young stallion. She is sending him back to the gypsy in England."

Without thinking I heard the words coming out of my mouth, "No! I want to buy this horse, Rudy, please!" "This is a stallion, you lack experience. I'll find you a horse that will be safe for you", he pleaded.

"If necessary I'll learn, you can teach me how to be safe. I want this horse." With a challenge in his voice I heard Rudy say, "Okay, take him for a walk." My excitement rose as I slid the stall latch, then I was standing next to this beautiful creature. He raised his head and I clicked the lead on and turned him to walk out into the aisle. He followed obediently.

We walked past the other stalls out into the sunshine. Rudy was telling me to go into the barn where the mares were. If I wanted a stallion I was going to have to manage him around mares. I really don't remember what all Rudy was saying; I was just walking "my" horse. We passed the mares; he quickened his step a little and raised his head, nothing unmanageable.

Once outside Rudy directed me to walk the horse towards the arena and between the parked cars. I did and brought him back without any problem. Rudy then took the lead from me and walked the horse a short distance up the road, turned and ran back with him. The mane and feathers were flying, the head held regally; the effortless trot made him seem even more unreal. When Rudy stopped him in front of me there were no questions. Yes, this was the horse I felt I had waited all my life to have. A smiling Rudy explained that we would have to convince the gypsy to sell to me. We put my beauty back in his stall and I followed Rudy to the office. He made the call explaining an American woman was interested in the stallion. He then handed the phone to me. I don't recall the conversation exactly. I spoke with a childhood joy how this horse had captured me. The gypsy seemed to understand; as he shared his horse was truly special. There are not many if any like him. The gypsy had not planned to sell the horse, since his friend did not want him. I thoughtfully responded, "I understand, just know that when he leaves and goes home to England he will take my heart with him." There was a long silence and the gypsy questioned, "He has your heart?" "Yes", I said. Another pause and then, "Well, if he has your heart he doesn't belong to me anymore, he belongs to you."

I had learned something of gypsy culture that day. I would come to know it is often much more about heart than the sale when it comes to the horses they treasure. I shook Rudy's hand; the deal had been made. I owned the horse; my horse; a beautiful special horse from the gypsies. Jill and I had been thinking of horse names for over a year, just in case we ever got another. One name in particular was a favorite, Bandit. It was a good name for him because if the truth is known this horse stole my heart from the very first moment I saw him. Today, I just tell people he is my heart.

Bandit, age three, with Jill in the Theisen's
courtyard shortly after we bought him.

Life in Biersdorf was good; the horses, friends, and the little house on the cul-de-sac. I was content. Of course when things become comfortable and routine seems to fit like a glove, life has a way of throwing us a curve ball. It was 1999 we were approaching the end of a century; the beginning of a new one. As an educator I was on a high. I had served as President of ASCD Germany and had been invited to be the guest speaker at the International Educators' Day in Brussels, Belgium. My presentation on "Future Schools", and dealing with change had won me professional accolades. Here I was teaching about inevitable change, how to accept change, not knowing that I would soon be dealing with significant change on a very personal level.

My daughters had spent their entire lives in Germany. In the summers we had visited relatives in Alabama; that was vacation, Germany was home. As they both were entering middle/high school I began to feel they should have the experience of not just visiting the United States, but living there. Also the restructuring of the Armed Forces in Europe was impacting the Americans residing in Europe and the schools serving those populations. US Army/Air Force communities which once had been the size of a small city found themselves now in many cases less than a village. Such was the case with Bitburg. With a decrease in student population I was told I would be reassigned to a school in Ramstein at the end of school year 2000-2001. As I contemplated this move, I began to think if moving was on the horizon then maybe this should be the time to move home to the United States.

I wanted to continue my career with the Department of Defense Schools and so I began to search for available stateside positions. I found an opening for Assistant Principal at the Elementary School located on the campus of the United States Military Academy at West Point, New York. I submitted my application fully expecting tough competition for such a prestigious place. Having little faith that anything would come of this I proceeded to plan for our move to the Ramstein area. The girls and I made a couple of trips searching for houses and of course boarding facilities for our horses. We located a really lovely country home. A boarding barn wasn't too far away, but it certainly could not compare to Rudy's place. Jill figured out it was too far for her to walk and began to plead for a Moped. With this she would have her own transportation to the stable after school. She wouldn't have to wait for me to drive her after work. All the pieces seemed to be fitting together nicely, making the transition appear less painful.

On a weekend trip to Ramstein, I signed the rental contract for the house and made all the necessary arrangements with the stable owner. The following week my plans were halted by an email from the Human Resources Officer for the West Point Schools. The message indicated I had made the first cut and was scheduled for an interview. Normally this would have been good news; however, I was starting again to feel comfortable with the move to Ramstein. After all we had a house and a stable, what more could I ask for or need. I told myself this interview more than likely was a formality and not an indication I even had a chance for the position.

The day of the interview arrived; the call came and I wasn't at all nervous. I didn't plan on getting the job, Ramstein was my destination. I enjoyed answering the questions and sharing with fervor my knowledge and expertise of early childhood education best practices. When I walked out of my office following the interview my boss and colleague was anxious to know how it went. I reassured her that all was well. I felt confident the interview was successful but this was West Point and I didn't feel I had done "that" well. I assured her I would still be in Germany when school resumed in the fall.

The next day a call came from the West Point Schools. The person on the phone was offering me the position of Assistant Principal. This wasn't supposed to happen; I was going to Ramstein, now I had to make a choice. I worried how my daughters would feel about such a drastic move. I struggled with whether this was the right time, the right step to take. Yet, something inside urged me to see this as an opportunity, one I should not let pass me by.

I decided to do an internet search and see what I could find out about West Point. The site was filled with beautiful images of the campus, cadets, historical buildings where Presidents had studied and generals had been born. The scenery of the magnificent Hudson River was beautiful. Then when I looked under their MWR (Morale, Welfare, and Recreation) section to see what fun things my girls and I would be able to do. I found "Morgan Farm".

West Point had a riding/boarding stable! I had been working for the government schools for a long time and none of my previous assignments had a riding stable. Now I was being offered a job at the USMA, one of America's most honored schools, AND it had a boarding stable for my horses. This was wonderful! My girls, what would they think of all of this?

Jamie, the oldest, had a boyfriend. She was going through that "I can make my own decisions and you aren't that important, mom" stage. When teenagers reach this point all you can do is hold on tight and hope the storm blows over quickly. Needless to say she was not a happy camper. The proposed move to Ramstein only a thirty minute drive down the road had already been a huge inconvenience for her. No, in her mind distance would not make the heart grow fonder.

Jill on the other hand was a willing supporter in the move. No, she did not want to leave her homeland of Germany, her wonderful group of friends and this lovely, nurturing, and comfortable little village. She was aware of Jamie's attitudes, anger, and resentment towards me for choosing to do this. She assured me she would never do those things. I hugged her often and knew in my heart her pain would not be while still on German soil, but rather once it was an ocean away.

We did not have much time to be flustered by this move. I received the job offer in early spring and had to report to West Point in July. Finishing the school year, making appointments for pack out and pick up of household goods and of course the arrangements for getting two dogs, two cats, and two horses all safely to New York filled my days.

Somewhere in there was the consoling, comforting, and encouraging of two teenage girls who saw parts of this as the end of their world. My heart though troubled knew the decision was also founded in what I believed would ultimately be best for all of us. The weeks that followed were hectic. Emotions were high; there were days when all three of us felt satisfied about this and began to think of good reasons for moving to the states. That could all change in an instant and feelings of sadness would flood the house with uneasiness. At which times I would want to crawl inside myself and wonder why on earth I was doing this.

Jill was spending as much time as she could at the stable while Jamie was always with the boyfriend. My "to do" list was overwhelming. I made arrangements for the movers to come; an appointment to ship the van; and of course the flight arrangements for our menagerie. The dogs and cats were easy. I called Pet Air and was able to get them out on the same morning as our flight. They would arrive safe and sound at JFK and be waiting in the cargo area when we arrived.

Preparing to move the horses to the USA was another story. While arranging for the dogs and cats I had learned Morgan Farm at West Point had a kennel as well as the stable. The manager of the facility was Peter Cashman. I knew he was probably having nightmares about this insistent woman in Germany who called him at least every other day. I had a million questions and I needed answers to them all. I was about to fly my beloved horses across an ocean and to a strange place where there would be few, if any, other horses like them. I knew they would be an oddity at Morgan Farm.

I was taking my daughters away from their homeland; I was leaving a country I had spent more of my life in it seemed, than the land of my birth. This was all unsettling. Yet I continued down this path unwaveringly. Rudy was wonderful and helped set up required vet appointments for Bandit and Magic's travel. Blood work had to be done at precise times within a certain amount of hours before they boarded the plane. Quarantine reservations had to be scheduled and flight arrangements made on the equine transport flying out of Bonn, Germany.

That school year seemed to close by itself. My life was a madhouse of boxes; paperwork; farewells; tears; and sleepless nights. Before I knew it July had arrived. Bandit and Magic were scheduled to fly the day before us. I will never forget that morning. The vet was supposed to come out with the required documents clearing them for the flight. We had to bathe them with soap and water and then with vinegar to hopefully rid them of any possible bacteria that could be transported. I always loved giving them a bath and using wonderful smelling horse shampoos. They always smelled so lovely after their bath. Today's vinegar bath left them smelling like a couple of pickles; it was strange.

Time was a precious commodity that day. We had to travel to Bonn which was several hours on the road. We had to be on time at the airport to be cleared for the flight. I was getting nervous because there was no window for error. Either the horses made the flight or I would be leaving them behind in Germany until I could rearrange a new flight. We were flying the next day and there was no changing a government ticket.

As the minutes flew and no vet was in sight, I ran in and out of Rudy's office phoning the doctor. We were right down to the wire when his truck pulled into the courtyard. He checked out the horses while I held my breath; there could be no problem at this point in this journey. Finally I held in my hand the necessary documents; said *Vielen Dank* to the vet while Jill and Rudy loaded Bandit and Magic on the horse trailer. Rudy, his daughter, Louisa, his son, Max, Jill and me climbed in the truck. We were on the road to Bonn.

Bandit and Magic were good travelers. You could barely feel them shift their weight occasionally. They were together quietly munching on hay. There was an excitement about the newness of this experience which somehow seemed to lessen my worry for a moment.

Once at the airport Rudy followed the carefully written directions to the cargo area. I thought we were going to the end of the earth; at least it seemed that way. We turned down narrow roads surrounded by high fences with barbed wire at the top. I determined no one was going to get out or in this place. Right when I thought we surely would reach a dead end the road widened a bit and a terminal of sorts was visible. Rudy stopped the trailer and told me to go in and let them know we were here. As I was walking to the door it opened and a nice young woman greeted me by name. I followed her in and motioned for Rudy, Louisa, Jill and Max to come in too. There was a large sitting area with sofas and chairs facing the windows looking out on the parking area for the trailers. I was given the red carpet treatment. As I signed paper after paper the attractive young woman was telling me how happy they were to have Bandit and Magic on the flight. She was sharing who would be on the flight with them and telling me the approximate arrival time in New York. I was told someone from their stateside office would give me a call once the horses safely reached their destination. They would then be taken to the quarantine center in Newburgh, New York.

We were at least two hours early, but I was glad for the extra time. I needed it for my head to clear. Rudy had brought *brotchen* with *wurst*. I watched as Jill, Louisa and Max were enjoying this favorite meal. I wondered if you could get good German *brotchen* and *wurst* in New York.

Suddenly I heard sirens from Politzei cars coming into the trailer area. There was one car with flashing lights and blaring siren followed by a very large horse van which in turn was followed by a second Politzei car. This caravan came to a halt right next to our little trailer.

There was an exchange between the nice young woman who had assisted me and people from the van. I saw papers, and the young woman was pointing with her fingers down another narrow road leading away from this terminal. Soon she returned to the waiting area. Another young woman and a man came through the doors. This woman said hello sharing that she was a handler on the flight. As if she could read my worry she explained there would be two veterinarians along with six handlers to serve the twelve horses on board. The ten horses that had arrived with police escort were show horses which had been competing in Europe. Their estimated value at a little over one million dollars gave need for the police protection.

With the arrival of the other handlers our little party was ready to proceed to the special hanger housing the equine transport plane. As our little group prepared to return to the trailer we were stopped and informed that no one under eighteen would be permitted in the hanger. A sad Jill, Louisa and Max had to remain in the waiting area while Rudy and I climbed back in the truck to follow the large horse van. One of the Politzei cars lead the way followed by the horse van, then our little trailer and the second Politzei car brought up the rear.

We wound down tight passages all lined with the same wire fence; Politzei lights flashing. Then we entered an airplane hangar. The police cars took up a guard position at each entrance. Rudy and I were told that the competition horses would be loaded first. The six handlers had their work cut out for them as these sleek; elegant sixteen to seventeen hand beauties with fire in their eyes came off the horse van. They reared, and side stepped, while shrill whinnies filled the air. I was only hoping Bandit and Magic were not becoming frightened by all of this. As the last of the big horses were loaded one of the handlers came over and said they were ready for us.

Now came the most fascinating moment. These young handlers had been demonstrating maturity and equine skill that was calming my worries and fears. It had been all business with those sixteen hand majestic creatures. Suddenly Rudy lowered the tailgate of the trailer and I backed Bandit off. Six handlers came running over, talking like eager children in a candy store; "Oh my gosh, look at him, isn't he beautiful!" Then came the, "Do you need help, do you think he will go in the container easily?" I said I believed he would follow me anywhere and that is just what my boy did. I walked him right into the container where nice fresh hay was more tempting than freedom.

We secured him and I returned to unload Magic to a repeat performance of drooling horse lovers. She too made me proud by walking into the container as if this was something she did every day and simply couldn't understand what all the fuss was about. After she was loaded and I stepped out they continued to ask questions about my two fluffy ponies and the vet came over and laughingly said he might have trouble getting them to remember there were twelve horses on the flight, not just two.

As we drove away I was thinking these special horses had given me yet another experience in life I would have completely missed without them. I smiled. We returned to the terminal to an anxious Jill who was sad she had not been allowed to help put her horses on the plane. No manner of sharing what had transpired made it any better. A disappointed Jill, Louisa, and Max joined Rudy and me in the truck for the return trip to Biersdorf. The morning would bring another day of travel. I closed my eyes while Rudy drove. I was tired.

The next morning arrived. We drove to Frankfurt International Airport making our first stop the Pet Air drop off. Here again we had to turn over our dear animal family members to attendants assuring us they were in good hands. Sofie, our shepherd mix, we had rescued while vacationing one summer in Italy, was calm and seemed okay with all that was going on around her. Then again, this was Sofie. Not too much frazzled her; unless she thought something or someone intended us harm, then she became the big bad guard dog. I also think she felt she had to set the example for MacIntosh, my precious West Highland Terrier, who was my shadow. I had never been too far from him since getting him as an eight week old puppy. Now I was putting him on an airplane. It was difficult to hand his carrier over. He barked, but then he seemed to take his cues from his friend, Sofie, who was resting quietly in her large kennel. Of course the two cats, Fonzie and Artemus, were loudly protesting this interruption in their day. They would much rather be at home in Biersdorf, sleeping on a bed or curled up on the sofa pillows. Instead they were crying and fussing about this trip they now found themselves taking. Wiping away a stray tear, I turned to check with the attendant to make certain I had all the necessary information as to where to check in with Pet Air once we arrived at JFK. Then we made our way to the people terminal and checked in.

It was an uneventful flight; we had made it so many times. We would go to visit family and friends in America and then return to Germany, this time it was one way. For the three of us it really had not become a reality as yet. We simply were on a plane flying to America.

Arriving at JFK I was tired and it was late afternoon. We departed the plane and found baggage claim. As we collected our bags they seemed to have multiplied. I simply did not remember we had this many. Yet there they were; all needing to be carried to wherever the rental car was located. We each gathered up as many items as we could; miraculously we had it all and managed to find our way out into the open terminal area where I began to look for the rental car signs. Ah there it was;

realizing I would need to exit the terminal to pick up the rental car I told the girls to just put the luggage down in a pile and to wait by it until I returned with the car. As I went through the revolving door I looked back at my daughters sitting on our worldly belongings. They looked out of place and sad. A feeling of uncertainty and homesickness was overcoming me. I tried to shake it off and proceeded towards the rental car area. A very friendly lady assisted me with the paperwork and soon I had the key to the Dodge Caravan that would carry my family the next few miles of our journey. I fortunately was able to park right in front of the doorway where I had left the girls and our things.

They did smile when they saw me and quickly helped load the van. I had asked the rental car lady for directions to the Pet Air arrivals. That was our next stop. As the sun was setting I pulled the van up to the cargo area next to what looked like a loading dock.

The large roll back door was ajar and as I looked beyond the entrance I noticed two dog kennels and suddenly a very familiar bark was heard. Yes, there they were my Sofie and Mac safe and sound and greeting us with friendly barks and wagging tails. A man came over and said, "I believe they know you." He took my paperwork and then brought the kennels over. He disappeared into the building returning with the kennel containing Fonzie and Artemus. With the help of the Pet Air attendant we loaded the dogs and cats. There literally was no more room in the van with us, the luggage, and all of our animals. I thanked the man and climbed behind the wheel to drive to West Point.

We crossed the Hudson River and went north on route 9W. The directions I had been given were excellent. I was glad. It was night; the girls were asleep as were the dogs and cats. It was quiet and I was driving in the dark headed towards the beginning of the next chapter of my life. Then there it was the sign for Highland Falls/West Point. I turned right and drove a short distance when I saw the Five Star Hotel on the right. This was the West Point Military Hotel for departing and arriving personnel. As I pulled into the parking lot and turned off the van I sat for a brief moment taking in the quiet and stillness. I said a little prayer of thanksgiving. We had made it; a safe and uneventful trip.

I left my sleeping girls and pets and went to the front desk. The lady smiled and had me sign in and handed me the room key. Not a lot of talk exchange as I know she could see I was exhausted. I did ask if there was a phone I could use to call Morgan Farm Kennel. Mr. Cashman had been kind enough to provide me with his home number. He had said it didn't matter what time we arrived, he would open the kennel for my animals. I dialed the number, a familiar voice answered. He would meet me at the kennel. After getting directions and hanging up I thanked the desk clerk and returned to the van. I gave the girls the option of going to the hotel room or driving over to the kennel. They decided to drive with me. It was a short trip, fifteen minutes at the most. As Mr. Cashman turned on the lights we were greeted with loud barking. We had definitely awakened the other boarders. A nice large kennel had been prepared for Mac and Sofie. They would share one and it seemed as if this pleased them. Fonzie and Artemus would also share a kennel in the cat room. Once our precious dogs and cats were safe I thanked Mr. Cashman and said good night. We returned to the Five Star where my daughters and I were most happy to find our room and climb into bed.

The next day I went to the window and realized the hotel was located on the banks of the beautiful Hudson River. It was a very nice peaceful view. We dressed and drove over to the post to find my new school. West Point at that time was an open post. We just drove right through Thayer Gate, passed central campus and finally arrived at West Point Schools. I checked in with the HRO office and chatted briefly with my new boss. After the school we drove around the campus and truly enjoyed its beauty and college atmosphere. Upon returning to the hotel I could sense Jamie was a bit out of sorts.

She did not wish to go to Morgan Farm that afternoon to check on the animals with Jill and me. So she remained at the hotel. Jill and

I went to the kennel and we took Mac and Sofie for a walk. We then took Fonzie and Artemus out of their kennel and let them explore the cat room for a while.

We met Mr. Cashman's family, his lovely wife, two daughters and son. We learned that his wife was a riding instructor and the girls both rode. They were all friendly and seemed to share our excitement about our horses arriving soon. In fact Bandit would be arriving in two days. He had to remain in quarantine for three days, but being a gelding he could then be released. Magic on the other hand was a mare, could reproduce, and thus was restricted to quarantine for three weeks. She had been sent to a special quarantine farm in New Jersey, All-D-Reiterhof, where we would be allowed to visit. Jill and I were already looking ahead and planning a weekend drive down to see Magic.

We had arrived in New York in July 2001. I came with two teenage girls. This alone was a challenge. When you add the fact they had been uprooted from the only country they had truly known, the people they loved, the friends and all things safe and comfortable to them; you can understand the pain that began to grow. When pain takes root in a teenage soul, unaddressed it often will sprout forth as anger, defiance or worse; withdrawal and depression. I knew my decision to make this move had created pain and difficulty for both of my girls; they would deal with this as individuals; as their mother I could only offer to help. Resentment led to seeking help through peers rather than a parent; therein was my pain. It would take time, support, and maturing to bring healing; and for each of us to recognize coming to America was good.

It soon became clear if any peace was to be had in the "getting settled" process, it would be necessary to send my oldest daughter back to Germany. So only a week after arriving I sent Jamie back to friends with the expectation she would return the week before school started here.

August 2001 was a blur. I was so very busy learning a new school community and my job responsibilities. Jill and I were living at the Five Star Hotel. She spent the majority of her day there while I went to school. In the afternoon we went to Morgan Farm and spent much desired time with our dogs and cats. This was my sanctuary.

Magic remained at All-D-Reiterhof to complete the quarantine. On our visit we found a lovely, well managed facility. All the horses were calm and content. It was obvious that each was given attention and wonderful daily care. After our visit I felt comfortable with Magic being there. Bandit had safely arrived at Morgan Farm following his three day quarantine.

He had traveled well except for a huge place on the top of his tail which in his anxious traveling moments he had rubbed raw. A few days of carefully cleaning, medicating, and gently wrapping that wonderful tail found it well on the road to recovery. We were truly happy to have Bandit back with us. Everyone at the farm loved him and Jill quickly made friends with the other girls and their horses. My stress was lessened by this and I saw a glimmer of hope at least for this daughter.

Jamie flew back the week before school began as planned, but not without difficulty. She missed her scheduled flight and I had to make other arrangements for her which added to the expense of this adventure. The expense was becoming a problem − a real problem. Before making the decision to accept the position at West Point I had been informed by the Principal and Human Resource Office that living in New York would be a costly undertaking. Many educators working for the Department of Defense saw West Point Schools as the ultimate assignment. The salary scale topped the list. However, no one realized why it was necessary for West Point staff to receive such salaries, until you came here. Now it was apparent without this compensation you could not afford even the bare necessities of life.

Jamie was back safely. I could release one point of worry and try to concentrate on finding a home for my family. I had decided not to look for horse property as my dream was to settle in the south upon retiring; only eight years away. My sister and brother-in-law had encouraged me to think about buying a house for investment purposes. I prided myself in my frugalness over the last fifteen years. I had a comfortable little nest egg and felt I could proceed with the search. However, I had set a limit to ensure finances were not all eaten up by home buying. I remember the first time I shared my set limit with my realtor. The look on her face was one of disbelief. As she began to show houses in that range I understood why. For the price I could buy a new three bedroom, two car garage house with in ground pool in Alabama, I could only afford a fixer upper in New York. This reality was quite alarming to me. The idea of renting just did not seem feasible with all of my animals. So, what I thought would be a fun house buying adventure turned quickly into a not so pleasant necessity. I was shown house after house in run down areas or in such need of repair it would not have been worth it.

All the while bills were piling up; hotel charges, pet boarding costs. What little money I was planning on saving and not putting into a house was fast being depleted by just day to day existing. Finally after three months of searching the realtor called to say she thought she had found a house for us. It was quite a distance from West Point, but she explained many people have learned to travel at least an hour's distance to be able to own a home here.

That very afternoon she picked me up and off we went to what I thought was the other end of the world – Port Jervis, New York. The location is beautiful. Port Jervis sits on the borders of New York, New Jersey and Pennsylvania where the upper Delaware River flows. As we entered the town I liked what I saw. It was calm and I liked the small town atmosphere. My realtor stopped her car in front of an adorable brick Cape Cod style house; for the first time I didn't cringe and quickly stepped out of the car. The house had been maintained well, or so it seemed. I loved the yard and could immediately envision Mac and Sofie playing there. I liked the floor plan and the house felt comfortable to me. As we said good bye to the seller and returned to the car I gave my realtor the nod. This was it, this would be home.

On the return trip to West Point I felt relieved and began to think about the next item requiring my attention – a place to board my horses. Even though it was tempting it would not be possible to leave them at Morgan Farm. Obviously Jill and Jamie would be attending school in Port Jervis and I wanted a stable where we could care for the horses daily as we had always done. Therefore we had to find something in or around the Port Jervis area. I don't remember who told me about High Point Training Center, but whoever it was I owe a debt of gratitude. It was located in High Point, New Jersey just minutes from Sussex, New Jersey and Port Jervis. Owned and operated by Nels and Anna Nelson, truly delightful horse people.

I drove out to see the stables. As I turned down the gravel driveway I noticed an attractive blond woman grooming a horse at the first of three barns. I stopped my car and inquired if boarding spaces were available. She said yes and I would need to speak with Nels. He was over at the other barn. I parked and walked over. A tall cowboy of a man was coming out of a stall. I introduced myself and explained my interest in boarding. We talked briefly and exchanged all the needed information. It was decided I could bring Bandit and Magic as soon as we were ready.

The drive back to West Point was nice. Finally I thought all the pieces were falling into place and none too soon. In November, 2001 we moved into our little house in Port Jervis. Mac and Sophie were delighted to have a backyard all their own. Fonzie and Artemus loved having their sofa and bedrooms available to them once again; making themselves right at home. I loved standing at the kitchen sink looking out the window and watching the dogs running and playing; or simply sleeping in the grass. High Point Training Center was only a twenty minute drive from the house, my horses were close and I could manage to fit their care into what would become a very busy schedule.

The first few months in the house were peaceful and enjoyed by us all. The girls I believed liked that we were somewhat removed from West

Point. September 11 had been a difficult reality. Its horror lingered in the minds of my teenagers who felt not only had their mother taken them from their homeland, but she also had brought them to a war zone. This little cottage of a house close to the beautiful Delaware River offered reassurance that loss and pain can be faced when there is love, faith, and hope, or so it seemed for a brief moment.

My days began at 4:30 am. I drove out to the barn to care for Magic and Bandit. We had set up rough board which meant I was responsible for all of my horses' care to include turn out, stall cleaning, feeding, and training. Nels and Anna watched with interest believing I wouldn't be able to keep this up for too long. Little did they know caring for my horses, spending time with them, hanging out in the barn and visiting with horse people was for me a time of relaxation and renewal. As the months passed this place of escape would provide moments of peace; help renew strength and give me the calm resilience necessary for me to face each day. I understood tragedy, disappointment, and upheaval in one's life could have many causes and rarely are we ever prepared when life takes such a course. Prior to coming to New York things had been rather common, uneventful, pleasant and rewarding; in other words comfortable. I know I certainly wasn't prepared for the Lewis Carroll turn my life was about to make. His Alice would become a frequent point of reference in my search for a return to normal, to a comfort level I had somehow left behind in Europe.

Jill and Jamie enrolled in Port Jervis High School. My schedule unfortunately left them on their own more than I liked. I had to leave for the drive to West Point between 6:30 and 7:00 each morning and then returning home at 5:30 in the afternoon. Then it was off to the barn; returning home around 7:30 or 8:00. Jill went with me at first. This barn had no one her age, in fact all the boarders were older adults; Western riders – reining horse folks. None of them saw anything great about our two chunky, hairy horses. Though I tried to encourage; she lost interest; she was becoming a teenager. Peers took precedent over Mom. Her trips to the barn were limited to weekends and finally even those stopped.

Soon I found myself being the sole caretaker for Bandit and Magic. I missed Jill's ability and skill. Without her I was forced to build stronger relationships with the horses. While I wanted Jill to remain involved I soon learned this was not something I could or should force. She would have to come back on her own.

Having already discovered riding was not going to be my strong point I decided it was time to learn the art of carriage driving and to honor my chosen breed's roots. While attending, "Driving Day" at the New Jersey State Fair Horse Show, a driving instructor was recommended. Her name was Susan Skipper.

I called Susan and explained I had a Gypsy Vanner gelding I wanted trained to drive. She was excited as she had attended a driving show in the south and had seen a Gypsy Vanner team. The pair was Jasmine and Esmeralda owned by Bill and Joanne Thorup.

Those mares were two of the original sixteen Vanners imported by Dennis and Cindy Thompson to establish the breed registry. The Thorups had been showing their mares throughout the United States and Canada. In 2001 they became the North American Tandem Driving Champions.

Susan was excited about being able to work with a Vanner. She explained her barn was small but she did have an opening. Within a few days I was standing at the back of the trailer ready to have Bandit disembark. Susan's husband, Adam, was next to me. When the trailer ramp lowered Adam's expression was one I had become very familiar with when people encountered Bandit for the first time. The jaw lowers in disbelief, then a wide pleasing smile while the voice is immediately declaring amazement over such an animal. This always made me happy as I knew from day one he was indeed special. His tail touched the ground yet he never seemed to step on it as he backed. His mane was braided and the braids were at his knees. Susan was impressed as she took him and lead him into the barn, with the rest of his entourage following.

I liked the way she took charge. It was going to be no nonsense and Bandit needed that. I could also see she saw what I had seen in this horse – something rare and truly special. Once he was settled we entered her kitchen and sat at the table, the first of many nice moments there. Susan explained her training plan. I would be trained along with my horse. The end result would be a partnership enjoyed by both. Due to my job driving lessons were scheduled for the weekends. With a lesson time in place I said good-bye to my boy knowing I was leaving him in the best of hands. It was October 2002.

Now, my morning duties at the barn took less time as I only had Magic. I was at first a little concerned she would miss Bandit terribly. They were very attached to one another. However, within a day or two she showed no signs of worry and was happy as long as the other horses in the barn remained. She was brushed and loved daily. I only wished Jill wanted this barn life as much as I had come to enjoy it. I looked forward to Saturdays, my driving lesson day! High Point was on the way to Hardwick, New Jersey where Susan lived. I'd do my barn chores; get Magic set for the day and head to Susan's. The first couple of lessons I was just the observer. Susan would demonstrate what she and Bandit had accomplished during the week. She couldn't get over what a quick learner he was. It seemed as if he had been internally programmed for this work. I learned to walk behind him and line drive him. I was so excited. The fast approaching winter months would force Susan to take him to North Winds Stables just a couple of miles away. They had an indoor arena and this would enable our training to continue no matter the inevitable cold and snow.

While Bandit was learning his job in this driving partnership; an American Standardbred mare named Simply was teaching me mine. I learned the many parts to the harness and how to get Simply ready to hitch to the cart. Susan was a firm believer in the "learn by doing" method. When riding the rider makes contact with leg, seat, hand, and uses the voice for directions and control. In driving it is all about holding the reins just right to maintain a gentle yet steady contact with the bit while using voice commands to guide and encourage the horse to walk or trot. The whip is an extension of the arm. It can gently touch the side or rear to encourage a move to either side or forward.

Simply was a great teacher. Susan coached from center arena as Simply and I made our rounds. Each weekend my confidence and skill grew until the wonderful day came when she told me that I would be driving my Bandit for the first time. He knew the drill; I knew what to do. I took the reins from Susan, she was smiling as I climbed into the seat and gave him the command, "Bandit, *allee* walk." Susan used French terms instead of the standard, "walk on" or "gee and haw". When he heard my command Bandit did as I asked and I was driving my boy!

All the while Jamie was doing well in school. Her grades were good; it was her senior year and she was looking forward to what her life could be following high school. Unfortunately Jill was having many troubles. I had long conversations with the counselors and her teachers. All agreed she was very smart but lacked motivation; she finished nothing. I did not know what to do. Nothing I said nor any manner of encouragement helped. She became defiant and angry. The friends she had chosen were involved with drugs. Skipping school or not going at all was their usual course. There were days when I would arrive at work only to receive a call from the school counselor letting me know Jill was not in school. I would then leave and head back to Port Jervis to try and locate her.

Sometimes I found her at home; other times I would not know where to begin to look for her. She was sixteen. After several such incidents it became necessary to enlist the help of the local police. They knew many of her friends well and cautioned me. I learned at age sixteen the NY laws allow an individual a great deal of freedom void of parental guidance. However, should the individual break the law, the parents could face charges. The Port Jervis police were compassionate. They understood the situation and obviously had helped others in such distressful circumstances. A file was created more on my behalf than Jill's.

Any time I did not know of her whereabouts; any time I had tried to get her to stay home or come home and she refused; I had to call the police for a record of this to go into the file. This would indicate later to a judge I had done all I could do.

Never in even my worst nightmares had I faced anything like the reality in which I found myself. I had to go to work, be professional, with the ever growing burden of my daughter's struggles suppressed during my work day. There were days when I did not know if she was alive or dead.

My closest friends urged me to sell the horses thinking it would relieve me of some responsibility. They simply did not or could not understand that my horses gave me the only sanity I could find in a world without reason. Brushing Magic, telling her my hurt and confusion gave me some comfort. She willingly let me cry into her mane; standing completely still as if to absorb my pain, I could see caring in her eyes. Finally releasing a long sigh or gentle snort, she let me know she understood.

My driving weekends with Bandit and Susan were complete escape. No one there need know my personal trials. Driving my horse renewed me and gave me hope; not just for me but for Jill as well. Deep in my heart I longed for Jill to come back to this simpler, less complicated life. I convinced myself the horses while they were my peace now; could one day be hers again.

Susan truly loved Bandit. He was like no other horse she had trained. Sitting in her kitchen following my lesson, we frequently discussed the Gypsy Vanner Horse. The internet was both God send and demon to this breed. Susan knew I solely supported the Gypsy Vanner Horse

Society, yet other websites had sprung up offering horses from the gypsies calling them Cobs and Tinkers. She was very confused. On one such afternoon she asked me if I was attending a meeting in Ohio for "all gypsy horse owners" in the United States. I confessed I knew nothing of it. Walking me over to her computer she showed me the announcement. I wrote down the phone number and told her I'd call to find out more.

On my drive home I let my mind retrace why I was so passionate about the name Gypsy Vanner Horse. I remembered the straggly, insignificant, black and white gypsy bred horses that came and went through Rudy's barn; I recalled my determination to understand Rudy's Buck and my Bandit; also, I knew I would never forget my joy in finding the Gypsy Gold website and my email conversations with Dennis and Cindy Thompson.

It was January 2003; sadly in July 2002 Cindy Thompson accidentally fell and died while waiting for her favorite mare, Darby Dolly to foal. Cindy's sudden and unexpected death had crushed her husband, Dennis.

In autumn 2002 he had talked of turning the registry over to the University of Florida. In his sorrow he struggled to keep the farm going let alone the registry. I had spoken with Cindy in June 02 asking about Magic's and Bandit's registration papers. She had explained they were behind in paperwork but she'd get them out to me as soon as she could. When I had not received the papers in early August, I called again. This time I spoke with a heartbroken and depressed Dennis, who told me of Cindy's death.

Now I was wondering who was responsible for this Ohio meeting and if Dennis was attending or even been invited. That evening I made the phone call. A man answered and was quite pleasant asking if I owned any gypsy horses. I replied that I owned two Gypsy Vanners. I asked if Dennis Thompson was attending. The voice became matter of fact and informed me that certainly Mr. Thompson was welcome if he wished to come. Knowing of Dennis' present emotional state I added I was planning on attending and if need be to represent the Gypsy Vanner Horse Society.

The meeting was to be held a couple of days prior to the Ohio Equine Affaire. I made my reservations and shared with Susan my concern over this. I confessed I had been somewhat oblivious to the websites popping up and more importantly what was being said on them. Horses were being imported into America that were gypsy horses, yes, but not Gypsy Vanner Horses.

The Thompsons had introduced the sixteen original mares and stallions at *Equitana* in Louisville, KY in 1998. Their Gypsy Gold website opened with the beautiful Gypsy King rearing in a crystal ball – and America fell in love. I completely understood this. However, Americans in general did not. They did not understand the culture that had developed this breed nor did they understand the British culture that in some ways had prevented the breed from being recognized as such. What they saw was a beautiful horse and as America is want to do – they wanted one – now – instant gratification.

The Thompsons spent four years and many trips to England, conversations with many gypsies and most importantly with a gypsy other gypsies referred to as "King of the Coloured Horses"; his name was Fred Walker. For a culture without a written history, less than respected in a country they called home; and preferred privacy and seclusion, to be able to learn from one so honored was indeed going to the source.

While Dennis and Cindy were sitting with Fred in his caravan learning about his work with the coloured horses, I was in Germany watching a steady stream of coloured gypsy bred horses as they passed through Rudy's barn. My questions grew out of those observations; Dennis and Cindy's questions were centered on how Cushti Bok came to be.

I knew most of the horses coming into Germany could be nothing more than crosses, at the same time Buck and Rudy's show team clearly were genetic proof that a breeding program of sorts was being conducted somewhere and that was what I wanted to understand.

At the same time the British equestrian community was beginning its love affair with coloured horses. Mind you, not coloured horses bred by gypsies but any horse of colour. In fact they generally accepted most coloured horses to be crosses. Colour was attained through cross breeding. There was no breed recognition and in fact crossing was accepted and encouraged to get the colour. Shows were established and enjoyed by those who fancied such horses. In 1995 a British equestrian, Edward Hart, wrote a book about the coloured horses of Great Britain. In his book he highlights that none of the coloured horses could be considered a breed, yet if he was to pinpoint the closest to a breed it would have to be the horses bred by the gypsies.

When I happily discovered the Gypsy Gold website it was a celebration for me. My joy was in finding someone else who had asked the same questions, but unlike me had been able to find answers. Fred Walker and his fellow gypsies knew what they had; they knew what they were doing. They understood their horses bred true, time and time again. Dennis and Cindy Thompson knew they had uncovered an actual breed of horse which was unknown and unrecognized outside of the gypsy community. For Fred and his like minded kinsmen the horses were not for outsiders. The horses they treasured, the ones they kept close, were a reflection of the family's work; a source of great pride.

Buck, Bandit and Cushti Bok had escaped their beginnings and had begun a journey to share who they were with a whole new world of admirers. This I clearly embraced and understood. Unfortunately, Rudy was a horse trader. While he appreciated the nice ones like Buck and others he kept for himself, he accepted any and all gypsies' coloured horses on his buying trips to England. Gypsies who enjoy making a living buying and selling horses were happy to make the sale. It wasn't about evaluating or separating the wheat from the chaff, it was just about buying and selling. Rudy wasn't looking to recognize and celebrate this amazing accomplishment of the gypsies. He was a German riding instructor, a horse trainer and trader, and this was simply business to him. He had found these horses to be easily maintained and managed. This was important to his riding school and stable. Like any horse person though, he knew he had a special horse in Buck; he knew ones like Buck could help him sell others whether the same quality or not.

Dennis and Cindy knew there was a breed. They wanted to not only recognize it, but establish a registry to record it, and of course they also saw this as an exceptional business opportunity. Naturally, they stood guard over access to their sources. They systematically imported and then introduced the breed. Their goal was to import only horses approved by Fred or others he had introduced to the Thompsons. Those imported horses would have a verbal history of sire and dam, when possible grandsire and granddam, but most importantly each would be from a well established selectively bred herd.

Horses therefore which could be registered with the Gypsy Vanner Horse Society would come into America through Gypsy Gold farm or be born from stock originating from Gypsy Gold. The beginning was a good one. As horses from the original sixteen were sold, their new owners were educated clearly on the breed, its history, and the importance of the name Gypsy Vanner Horse. These new owners were the beginning to honoring and establishing this newly recognized breed for *the very first time anywhere in the world.* However, once the Gypsy Gold website opened and people saw these horses for the first time, they wanted one. While many started at Gypsy Gold, others felt if the Thompsons could go to England and buy horses from the Gypsies then so could they.

I am convinced there are two keys to open *Pandora's Box,* one is the desire for money and the other is a craving to be first. These were my concerns as I continued my drive home and considered attending the meeting in Ohio.

April 2003 arrived and I was in Columbus, Ohio to attend a meeting for any and all folks in North America who owned horses bred by gypsies. I learned a few days before leaving for Ohio that Dennis Thompson would be attending. I was very happy. I had never met Dennis in person and I looked forward to seeing him.

I ate breakfast in the hotel restaurant and then went to the conference room for the meeting. There was a table set up where all attendees were to sign in. I noticed Joanne Griffin right away. Joanne and her husband Stephen owned Emerald Winds farm in Connecticut. They had imported horses and begun a breeding business. I had visited their farm to see one of their stallions, Stranger. They owned a lovely mare, Beauty, who I admired. I signed in and found a seat about mid way near the back. I wanted to be where I could see most of the people and watch reactions.

I heard a familiar voice, it was Dennis. He came in along with several ladies. They were chatting and moved over to the far side to find their seats. I got up and approached Dennis to introduce myself. He was happy to see me and gave me a hug. He then turned to join his group and I returned to my seat.

I recognized Jeff Bartko as the meeting was being called to order. He and his wife, Christine, were originally importers of Shire horses and now had begun to import horses from gypsies. Their business was Black Forest Shires and their website was one Susan had pointed out to me.

They imported large numbers of horses. The horses they brought in ranged from lesser to very good quality. This reminded me of how Rudy did business and I was frustrated. While I could see what Rudy was doing and why within the framework of the European cultures he did so, I could not understand why an American based business would not choose to mirror Gypsy Gold. Jeff introduced Sid Harker and Michael Vines, two Gypsies. I was very happy they were there. The discussions began and were from time to time heated.

I realized everyone who made the effort to attend this meeting came with their own purpose and desire for the breed as they saw it. Therefore, what I share is from my perspective derived from my purpose which was to represent the Gypsy Vanner Horse Society and defend its founding principles. From visiting multiple websites prior to going to Ohio I have to say I was on the defensive. I found on those sites poor quality animals being proclaimed as excellent. Some individuals had gone to the UK and aligned with a gypsy family declaring to have been raising "these" horses for generations. The American with the need "to be first" or wanting "to make a quick profit" saw this alliance as a means to those ends. Indeed *Pandora's Box* had been opened and this meeting was only the beginning of the troubles this breed would have to endure as a result.

So, as I sat near the back in the middle I was prepared for the games to begin. I only voiced my opinion as I felt it was needed. Obviously my comments were of interest because at a break, the two gypsies, Mr. Harker and Mr. Vines made their way to me. I smiled and introduced myself. I proudly produced photos of Magic and Bandit and shared my understanding of the breed from my German based experience.

In return, their expressions validated once again, that what I knew and hoped for the breed was right. Therefore, for two days I listened, defended my personal position, and witnessed this *Pandoric* display. I was disappointed in Dennis. All who wished to present to the group were given the opportunity. I had hoped when Dennis took the floor it would be to convince this crowd of his personal journey to understand the gypsy culture; how he and Cindy had come to recognize the gypsies' treasured horses as a breed. I wanted him to openly share that not ALL gypsies were involved in the breed's development; to clarify that most if not all do raise horses, primarily to support the meat market. Most do not have a breeding plan, but simply breed what they have to what they can find. The few, yes few families, who were breeding towards what Fred Walker called his vision horse also had horses they sold for very little as well.

The difference was they held back a selective herd with long awaited traits. These were not for sale; if one should be offered the price would be an indication of this family's hard work enabling this treasured animal to be possible.

This is what I was waiting for Dennis to proclaim! To help this diverse and separated group come to an understanding of why the GVHS simply could not, dare I say, should not accept any and all gypsy bred horses.

Instead he stood and pushed a Gypsy Gold display stand to the front. Making a marketing effort to convince all of us that through Gypsy Gold products the breed would gain prominence and we all would be winners. This was the wrong crowd for this presentation.

In this group were individuals already angry that they had not been first; already analyzing everyone there to see how they could best position themselves to take the lead away from Gypsy Gold or at least somehow level the playing field.

It was interesting to observe the reactions of Sid Harker and Michael Vines. This was not just the beginning of a new equine industry undertaking for Americans, but America was now a whole new market for the gypsy culture's natural inclination towards horse trading, wheeling and dealing if you will.

If indeed they loved the treasured horse, they surely could see what was on the verge of happening here; also, if they were interested in horse trading then opportunity had just knocked loudly.

One evening Michael Vines offered a presentation on the breed and the gypsy man's standard of excellence. I knew this would be a chance to see which way he was leaning. It would be the first time I had heard an actual gypsy discuss his breed. I arrived at the conference room early. I wanted a good seat and anticipated a large group in attendance. To my disappointment less than ten or certainly no more than a handful of people came. I did not see Dennis or any of the ladies. No matter I was there to listen and learn. There was an enthusiasm in Michael's manner. He appeared somewhat shy in the beginning, but as he talked he projected a confidence only a dedication to this horse could generate.

51

He discussed conformation from the sweet head to the tip of each feathered hoof. He loved these horses.

His presentation was unpretentious and informative. I felt sorry for and ashamed of others who had not seen this as an opportunity to learn or at least show respect for this young gypsy, no matter who invited him.

I saw no success in this Ohio meeting. It had been like having Microsoft and Apple trying to agree on forming one company. I did however feel I had learned much about what was already happening with the breed in the states and fearful of what was ahead.

I had lived mass importation of gypsy bred horses in Germany. In my opinion that had happened because of horse trading and no one caring to recognize the variety of gypsies' coloured horses. Within that hodge-podge were the Bucks and Bandits representing a small percentage of the total horse population bred by gypsies; the select herds of a few. Until Cindy Thompson began a love affair with a little stallion named Cushti Bok, those horses went unrecognized and uncelebrated as a breed.

The establishment of the Gypsy Vanner Horse Society with sixteen selectively bred horses and the opening of the Gypsy Gold website turned the spotlight on the gypsies' treasure and gave the Thompsons a unique place to share Fred Walker's story.

With that said I felt little if anything had been accomplished at this meeting. A committee was elected from all groups present to take a look at what had been discussed and agreed upon with the hope of forming one registry for the breed. Though the committee was formed it never convened. Dennis had stated he would open the GVHS registry to all horses who met the standard; even if their heritage was not known. While at the time this appeared to be an appropriate move this decision would also unfortunately enable questionable genetics into what had been established as a purebred registry. This would happen as a registration process was begun with inadequate education for the volunteers who wished to do the work. It would create future obstacles for the GVHS. At least the meeting attendees agreed the GVHS Breed Standard was the standard of quality they all hoped to achieve.

Thursday arrived and with it the opening of Ohio Equine Affaire 2003. I had breakfast in the hotel gathered my things and as I walked through the lobby I was greeted by Sid and Michael. They asked if they might ride with me to the expo grounds. I smiled saying of course and we walked to my rental car, climbed in and chatted about my Bandit on the trip over. Once there, they thanked me and were off to find their friends and I went to the Breed Pavilion.

Dennis had invited me to help in the GVHS Booth. I was delighted to meet Anne Crowley, Collette Morgan, Brenda Moore, Jeanne MacDonald, Mary Beth and Kristen Kerwin. All had come to assist Dennis and work in the booth. They had done a lovely job of decorating the area with pictures and gypsy artifacts – lots of black and gold gave it a rich and appealing flare. Dennis had brought his stallions, The Gypsy King and The Roadsweeper, as well as the yearling colt, B. B. King to represent the breed.

At nine o'clock sharp the doors opened and welcomed an eager crowd. The Vanners were indeed a fascination. I recognized the awe and was happy to share when questions were asked. I knew the questions; I knew the answers. This was familiar territory and I was confident of my knowledge of this breed. Understanding Bandit and his family had been my passion for seven years now and I was thrilled to be able to help introduce interested individuals to the horses that had changed my life.

In the afternoon, Dennis came by the booth after being out and about conversing with everyone. He invited me to come with him so he could introduce me to as he put it, "another school teacher". We walked across the width of the pavilion and came to a booth with a stall occupied by Dennis' Roadsweeper. The lady stood and was introduced as Jacki Clark. On a small table next to her chair was a small hand printed sign with the words, "Lash's Lessons". She invited me to join her and we immediately formed a connection and friendship. I learned from Mrs. Clark, she and her daughter, Stacy Foncannon, operated Shirecrest Equine Education Center in Kentucky. They had Lash, the first Gypsy Vanner Horse colt born in America. Since Lash was not with them, Dennis had offered The Roadsweeper to occupy the stall. It was very nice having a Vanner on either side of the Breed Pavilion.

Mrs. Clark shared her idea of a children's program featuring Lash. Being an elementary school teacher I was very excited about what this program could do for America's children. Over the course of Equine Affaire I spent much time with Mrs. Clark and shared her enthusiasm as we discussed her character ideas and potential for her program.

I also had the opportunity to meet Gypsy Gold's trainer and manager, Linda Pepple. I truly admired her knowledge and skill taking care and helping these stallions and young colt exhibit their best behavior throughout the event. She had no way of knowing how happy she made me one day when she handed me B.B. King's lead and allowed me to walk him around. I loved this colt. He was all black with white blaze and four white feet like Bandit. There were few if any other such marked Vanners in America at this time and therefore, he was a favorite of mine.

Sunday came much too quickly for me, but I had made new friends, affirmed my convictions to what I felt was right for the breed and looked forward to supporting other events with the Gypsy Vanner Horse Society and my Vanners.

Upon my return Susan was anxious to hear about the meeting. I shared with her my disappointment in much of what had transpired, but my pleasure in making new Vanner friends during Equine Affaire. We resumed my driving work with Bandit. He and I were becoming the team Susan had promised. There was nothing I enjoyed more. As spring turned into summer 2003, Susan began to suggest horse shows for Bandit and me to attend. The Warren County Show was coming up in July. Susan wanted to bring Caitlin, her twelve year old driving student also.

I wanted very much to show Bandit, but my confidence in managing him away from familiar territory was lacking. As I look back I realize Susan knew a show experience would be what was needed to push this chick out of the nest. Bandit and I had become working partners. I knew this. I wasn't ready to leave the safe haven of Susan's lessons and Saturday afternoon kitchen chats.

We worked with Warren County being our goal. The day arrived and Susan, Adam, Caitlin, and I were so excited. We arrived at the show grounds early, wanting to take the horses on a walk and introduce them to these new surroundings. This would let them meet anything scary before they encountered it on the way to or in the show ring. No surprises; just doing the job well, was all we wanted.

It was here that Susan forced my independence, while she worked with Caitlin. I was on my own. I took Bandit for his walk. He did look beautiful; Susan had maintained all of that hair wonderfully, and show comers admired the overall effect. People stopped us wanting to touch, pet and ask about this unusually striking horse. He loved the attention. The only scary obstacle we came across was a water hose stretched across the road. Bandit saw it and side stepped. I smiled, talked softly, let him examine it, and encouraged him to step bravely over it. Onlookers giggled. Other more spirited horses were whinnying loudly and prancing nervously as owners were prepping them for the show. Bandit was the quiet observer, he trusted me on this adventure. My mind flashed back to Alabama summers and horse shows long ago. Today a dream was coming true, I was showing my horse.

We returned to the trailer where Adam, Susan's husband, was waiting. Susan was with Caitlin about to enter the ring for one of the youth classes. Adam was there to assist me in getting Bandit harnessed and hitched. I managed on my own under Adam's watchful eye. Bandit stood quietly while I retrieved my hat, gloves and driving apron from the trailer.

As I lifted the reins and stepped into the cart, my quiet obedient horse awoke. He tried to rear and began to back up quickly slamming the cart and me into the trailer. Yes, while Susan and I loved this horse's quiet gentle nature, we also respected his moments of refusal and stubbornness. We referred to them as "Bandit moments". This was such a time; it frightened me. Adam tried to reassure me that it was over, but I begged him to ride in the cart with me as a groom. He did. I gave Bandit the command to move out and we were on our way. As we passed the stands heads turned and I heard the muffled approvals and praises. I smiled with pride as I drove my boy into the ring joining a group of eleven entries.

I felt Bandit look to the horse coming up on our right and then to the one on his left. Almost as if he thought, "Oh, this is what we are here for; let me show you all how it is done". He went perfectly into the bit and I felt complete control at the reins. I could not help but grin from ear to ear, my fine boy was pulling his cart perfectly and Adam and I were lucky enough to be along for the ride. Before I knew it we were lining up in front of the judge as directed. No thought of placing had entered my mind. This was my very first horse show and Bandit's too. I was pleased we had completed the task at hand in a successful manner. While these thoughts flooded my brain, the announcer was calling out the winners. He began with fifth place.

Maybe somewhere in my sub-conscience I hoped for fifth or fourth, but that didn't happen. I was beginning to relax and think about our next class, when to my surprise I heard the announcer saying, "…and first place goes to number 121, Joyce Christian driving Bandit." I was frozen. Adam who was heading Bandit leaned over and said, "That is you". He joined me in the cart and we drove over to get our ribbon, prize and made a victory round.

We then re-entered the ring for the Reinsmanship Class. I had just had the most delightful Cinderella experience. This second class was just for fun, nothing else mattered. As we lined up to face the judge I was still basking in our previous win when I heard to my truly amazed ears the announcer say, ".....and first place goes to number 121, Joyce Christian, driving Bandit." This time I heard the crowd. They were cheering at the top of their voices as tears of complete joy flowed down my cheeks.

As we left the ring and drove by the stands the crowd stood applauding and whistling as we passed. I pulled the cart up to the trailer where Susan and Caitlin were waiting. Susan saw my tears and gave me a big hug as she said, "Gee, do you think you can do this on your own now?" We all laughed. Caitlin had done well also and it was a time of celebration as we all loaded the trailer and headed home.

Within a couple of weeks I had made arrangements to take Bandit home. Susan and Adam had become such good friends. I would always remember the journey we had taken together with my Bandit and the fairytale day we had at the Warren County Horse Show.

My troubles with Jill had not improved over time. If anything they had worsened. When the school year came to a close it became increasingly difficult to keep tabs on her. Even though I worked in a school my job was year round. So, my schedule remained and suddenly she had all her time free. Yes, she had frequently skipped school, but the school always called and I had some idea of what was happening. Now with complete freedom, it was a disaster. She had become more rebellious and defiant.

In February after cutting her arms in several places she had been sent to Four Winds Hospital, a facility for troubled adolescents and teens. In my opinion her two week stay was not enough. However, all the testing simply revealed an unhappy, but normal girl. They found no tendencies outside the realm of what was perceived to be ordinary. I talked at length with the psychologist who found Jill to be an enigma. He recommended I have her see an adolescent psychiatrist to help her through her struggles whatever she saw them to be.

I made multiple calls to try and get her scheduled but the two psychiatrists in the area were full and recommended I have her see a counselor or social worker instead. They felt her problems were not severe enough and their caseloads were heavy. Here I was again down the rabbit hole. I had a recommendation from a respected facility, yet neither doctor could see a need to help my daughter. I had already tried a social worker. That had helped briefly but then Jill shut down; made fun of going and did not improve. She had wrecked my van with several of her friends in it. None of them had insurance. All of this was continuing to add to my already stretched finances.

I felt my world had been turned upside down with no way out. I was tired. My little cottage of a house that at first I was so happy to find had been vandalized by this group of misfit teenagers. A pool table was a gift at Christmas hoping to provide an incentive to stay close to home. Never would I have thought it would be an instrument of destruction. Yet, they had poked holes in my den ceiling with the pool cues and then broken the cues.

They had walked on my roof, causing leaks, and broken windows to get in the house when I had locked them out. The file at the police station had grown quite large and two policemen and I knew each other by first names. They truly were wonderful and every time there was an issue they exhibited sincere support and concern. They did not know what to do anymore than I did. I could not file charges because I had not actually seen the kids do the destructive things to my home, and in court it would be their word against mine.

As time passed I realized all of this was terribly wrong. If anything the law made it possible for these teenagers to get away with a multitude of sins. At the same time I could find no law that helped me in this situation. It was maddening. With my daughter able within the law to make her own choices and refuse to follow my guidance, she slipped further and further away from me. Yet, at every brick wall she hit, there was a return home.

It was August 2003 and she was on one of those returns when home didn't seem so bad. I had no way of knowing the worst was about to happen. Her current group all smoked and I was sure did a variety of drugs. Many of them had been kicked out of their homes. Having been living this for a while now, I understood those parents' decisions. How truly wrong was all of this? I struggled daily trying to find some answer or a means of reclaiming my daughter.

She now had a boyfriend. He was a very sad case; he'd been kicked out of his home; then been kicked out of a room in a friend's house. I believe he slept on the streets some nights. Jill had asked if he might sleep in our den on the sofa when he had no place else to go. I said he could and put a blanket and pillow in the hall closet for him to use on those nights. I told Jill I expected her to sleep in her room. She had complied with that request.

I was living in parallel universes while circumstance moved me from one to the other. In late July I received a phone call from Rich Hammler who worked with the New Jersey State Fair Horse Show. He had been to Florida and met the Thompsons and seen their Gypsy Vanner Horses. He had asked Dennis if it would be possible for horses from Gypsy Gold to attend the NJ State Fair and introduce the breed in the northeast. Dennis had told him there was no need for them to come up from Florida as I was nearby and could do it. Therefore, Mr. Hammler invited me to do a Gypsy Vanner Horse demonstration each evening for the event. We would also be the guests of Kistler Buildings and occupy their display stalls hopefully attracting the crowds. I was pleased Dennis had such confidence in me and my horses and I happily accepted this invitation.

I called Susan and she agreed to work with Bandit and drive him for the demonstration since I would be busy coordinating the demo. I asked Jill if she would ride Magic for the demo and she agreed to help. This made me very happy. She returned for this brief time to the barn to prepare; not every day but a couple of times a week.

One evening Mr. Hammler called with a question. He had received a phone call from, as he put it, "a woman in New Jersey who said she had gypsy horses and wanted to bring them to the fair for people to see."

He explained she would have to coordinate with me as the point of contact for the Gypsy Vanner Horse demonstration. I asked him if her horses were registered with the Gypsy Vanner Horse Society. He said he did not think so, but her name was Lise McNamara.

I called Dennis to see if he knew her. Indeed, he did. He and Cindy had visited the McNamara farm and Cindy had been so fond of one of the mares they had allowed a breeding to Cushti Bok even though Mrs. McNamara had not at the time registered her horses. He explained she owned very desirable breeding stock and he hoped she would at least register the colt by Cushti Bok.

Once again I was upset with Dennis. He was always so adamant about not breeding to stock outside the registry and yet he had done this and not followed up to make certain the horses were registered properly. I told him I was going to visit Mrs. McNamara and see if I could get her to register at least the colt.

After speaking with Lise on the phone and asking if I could come see the colt, my oldest daughter Jamie and I drove to West Milford, NJ, the following Sunday afternoon. We turned down the private driveway and followed it past the house and down to the beautiful twin barns. It was raining steadily as I stopped the truck in a parking space. I saw someone at the entrance to the first barn and told Jamie she did not need to come out in the rain. I think she was grateful for that option. She wasn't at all interested in horses, but had come along to keep me company and help with the directions.

I ran through a couple of puddles and shook off the excess water as I entered the barn and said hello. Lise greeted me and pointed out the precious colt with his stunning dam in the stall right next to us. They both were beautiful. Lise explained that Miss Tinkerbell was a McCann bred mare and one of her favorites. The colt was adorable and mostly white. She had named him Merrow. Since his mom was named for a fairy he had to be as well. Lise invited me into the stall and Merrow gave in to his curiosity to check me out. I was delighted as this was the first time I had been in a stall with a mom and baby before and it was great fun.

After playing with the foal she then took me on a tour of the barns and showed me a truly remarkable herd of Gypsy Vanners – yes, every horse was a Vanner, was selectively bred and wonderful examples of the breed. They all needed to be registered. Sitting on a bale of hay she shared that her first gypsy bred horse was the mare, Lady Wisteria, which her husband Steven had purchased for a birthday present. The mare had been purchased from Jan Anderson, a lady from Minnesota who had imported horses from the Robert Watson herd in England.

Lise and Jan had become very good friends and had formed a partnership to import and breed horses. As the afternoon wore on, I shared with her my passion for the breed and why I felt her horses should be registered with the Gypsy Vanner Horse Society. I told her I would be thrilled to have her join me at the NJ State Fair, but to do so the horses would have to be registered since my demonstration was representing the GVHS. I also explained that whether she chose to register all of her horses or not she should at least register Merrow. His sire was America's first Gypsy Vanner stallion and I encouraged her to honor that connection. She agreed to register not just the colt, but to my delight all of her horses.

As I rejoined Jamie in the truck for the ride home I was very happy. Not only had I been able to ensure that a Cushti Bok son was properly registered, but I had found another gypsy herd to admire and learn about. I felt it had been a productive rainy Sunday afternoon. I also had a new friend.

I contacted Dorothy Cleary in Pennsylvania to see if she would be interested and able to bring her beautiful Vanner filly, Heart of Gold, to participate in the demonstration. She agreed and as time grew short before the opening of the fair, I was very pleased with the plans for the introduction of the Gypsy Vanner Horse at the 2003 NJ State Fair Horse Show.

Susan would drive Bandit, Jill would ride Magic, Heart of Gold would be shown in hand and Lise had suggested her ten year old daughter, Kelsey, would ride their mare, Fiona. There would not be much time to practice but we believed if the horses went around the arena and lined up in the middle it would be sufficient. We knew the crowd would be spell bound over just their magical look.

"You must do the thing you think you cannot do."

Eleanor Roosevelt

The day came. I had to go to work, but planned on leaving around noon to get to the fairgrounds; set up; and make sure we were all ready. Shortly after eleven o'clock everything changed.

My secretary called me to the office for a phone call. It was the Port Jervis police; I was needed at the station immediately. They had Jill. I heard the officer saying, "…..Ms. Christian Jill's friend died in your den this morning……" I went white and slumped into the overstuffed chair in the office waiting area. Shock overcame me. I don't remember hanging up the phone. I asked my secretary to get me some water. She went into the kitchenette as the principal and supply clerk came in to see what was wrong. They were supportive yet concerned. When my secretary returned with the water I took a sip and somehow found my voice. Without details, I explained Jill was with the police and I needed to go to her. This was not an unusual request. They had heard it before, their worry was for me. My reaction was different this time and they cared. I assured them I could make the drive home. How, I don't know, but I did. I arrived at the station. Again the Port Jervis police were incredibly kind to me. There sat my daughter, with an empty, lost look on her tear stained face. My heart ached for her. I did not know how to help this child who was fast becoming a young woman.

One of the officers who had been assisting me with Jill for some time took me aside. He explained an autopsy would be done; they were suspecting an overdose. He asked me what I knew. I heard my voice respond, but it didn't sound like me, it sounded distant and far away. I tried to remember. The night before I heard Jill and Ryan come into the house late. Again, this was not out of the ordinary. After a while I heard Jill come upstairs and go into her room. In the morning after returning from the barn, I walked through the den as always to let the dogs outside. I heard Ryan make a moaning sound, but ignored this as common place. I went on about the morning routine. When I went back to the den to get the dogs in Jill had come down and was lying on the floor next to the sofa talking with him. I asked if he was okay. She was short, curt and disrespectful as usual. So, I finished getting ready to leave for work.

Remembering all of this, I began to sob uncontrollably into the officer's shoulder. How could I have prevented this from happening, why had I not seen that there was a problem? Why had I let the rude, coarse responses from my daughter keep me from pressing the issue? The officer tried his best to console me. Assuring me what had happened was accidental; maybe unavoidable. For now I needed to see to the care of my daughter.

She was released to me and asked if I would take her to Jen's house, telling me there were friends there who would understand. None of this seemed real to me so I did as she asked.

About a month before I had been encouraged by the police to think about moving out of Port Jervis for my family's sake. I had attended an equine health meeting with a friend and she had introduced me to Lynn Odendahl. Mrs. Odendahl owned a horse farm. Her barn had a three bedroom apartment in it. I had visited and thought it would be wonderful, but I had to sell my house first as I could not afford to pay my mortgage and rent. Given today's situation, the move was inevitable.

I had to get in touch with Mr. Hammler and try and do something about the fair. Jamie encouraged me to go ahead and try and take Jill to the fair; get her away from the situation, give her a chance to think about something else, even if just for a moment. I returned to Jen's house and spoke with Jill. She willing came with me as she had found her friends were not all kind nor did they see her as blameless. It is difficult to find the right words to capture this moment in time. It was pain; it was empty; it was filled with a great sense of loss; unnecessary loss. All our actions were as if someone else was doing them. At the fairgrounds Dorothy and friends had set up the camper and were ready. We had arranged for the camper so we could remain at the fairgrounds with the horses throughout the event. Heart of Gold was as beautiful as her pictures. Lise had arrived with not one horse, but three; Fiona and another mare with a foal at her side. There were three stalls in the Kistler display which had been provided for us and one stall in the show barn had been reserved for our group. Bandit, Magic and Heart of Gold(lovingly called Razzle) filled those stalls. I had planned to have the horses rotate out to the show barn stall to give each a rest from the crowds. Once Lise understood the plan she took the mare and foal home and the lovely Fiona remained.

The crowds did come. Kistler was not disappointed; yet I fear the people were not looking at the stalls but rather the horses housed in them. There was an air of excitement and fascination; all those feelings that come upon seeing something for the first time.

The horse show was well underway. About thirty minutes before our first demo, Susan and Adam arrived and took Bandit to prepare him. Rich came over to see if we were ready and to get a copy of the demo script to be reviewed. He returned within minutes with the approved script asking if I wanted the announcer to read it or was I? I said I would like to read it.

As I opened the door to the announcer's booth, I looked over my shoulder to see Bandit all decked out with his cart and Susan at the reins; ten year old Kelsey on Fiona, a prancing but controlled Razzle being lead by her trainer, and then my Jill sitting on Magic. This was the way life was supposed to be; yet, a cruel and unbelievable reality awaited us beyond the lights and fanfare of this brief beautiful moment in time.

I was welcomed by the announcer who introduced me and I began, "Ladies and gentlemen tonight I have the great pleasure to introduce a rare, new breed, the Gypsy Vanner Horse....." Susan entered with Bandit skillfully guiding him around the arena, and between jumps set up for the Grand Prix. He seemed to float as they made the rounds to a most appreciative crowd. Then Jill and Kelsey performed on those incredible mares followed by the precious Razzle who equally enjoyed her moment in the spotlight.

Left to right: Kelsey on Fiona, Heart of Gold with her trainer, Jill on Magic, and Susan driving Bandit (Photo courtesy of Reflections Photography, Inc. Kingston, NY)

With my closing remarks I dedicated this very special moment "..... to Jill's friend, Ryan, who had died suddenly today. He was in many ways a gypsy in search of a home. He will be missed, he was loved." Just as the audience had been loud with praise they responded to my closing words with a complete moment of silence.

Somehow, we made it through the next few days. Somehow, Jamie and I loaded a Penske moving truck multiple times and managed to get everything to the barn apartment at Lynn Odendahl's farm. It would be our second home since moving to NY.

As I recall this journey I find indeed that is exactly what it has been – a journey. Heritage Farm located outside of Walden, NY was simply the next stop along the way. Its owner, Lynn Odendahl, ran a bed and breakfast in her home. Many in this historic corner of the northeast operated B&B's and tourists were most grateful. In a quaint and charming atmosphere the tourist experienced the past while enjoying the comforts of the present.

Driving from the main paved street up the tree lined dirt road for a quarter of a mile or so you first noticed the brown plank house to your left, a tree adorned lawn with pond below was inviting to say the least. The road continued to curve around the house and found you facing the red metal twin aisle barn. The apartment windows looked out from above.

To reach the apartment you entered the left aisle and found a set of stairs just before the barn office. At the top of which was a wide area, once used as hay storage; its railings guarded each aisle and allowed for open viewing below. The apartment door was towards the back. I chose the two stalls opposite the stairway for Bandit and Magic. I could walk out and look down easily to check on them. They were the only horses in the barn except for Lynn's Thoroughbred gelding, Squirt. He was the last of her breeding program that once stood a son of Seattle Slew.

The apartment was spacious and quite comfortable. Lynn had recently renovated it. Our dogs and cats seemed undisturbed by yet another home. As long as their people were there they seemed satisfied.

The lawn down to the pond and the winding dirt road made great places to walk the dogs. Fonzie, the cat, explored the barn and enjoyed this extended freedom while Artemus, our scaredy cat, preferred the safety he found under my bed.

I loved the design of this barn. The aisles just beyond the barn office opened into the indoor arena, though smaller than the one at High Point, it was sufficient. On cold, rainy or snowy days I didn't even have to go outside. I could work the horses or turn them out to play in the arena while I cleaned their stalls. There was room at the front of the barn for my WARCO cart. Soon Bandit and I began to enjoy driving down the road and around the driveway that circled a tree covered knoll. I'd warm him up in the arena then drive down the barn aisle and out into the sunshine.

I had sold my house at a loss; my debt was building yet I found a feeling of peace at this quiet farm. I enrolled Jill in Central Valley High School, but not for long. We met with a wonderful support team of school counselors, administrators, and a school psychologist. They truly would, I feel, have given her careful attention and support if she had but given them the chance. A few days into the school year she refused to go. No amount of encouraging could convince her otherwise. I worried about leaving her alone but again I had to work for a living and at least she was farm bound.

We had been there only a short while when Lynn asked if I would have any problem if she allowed a trainer who had once worked out of her barn to return. Of course I did not object; I enjoyed having horse people around, learning from them, and sharing my horses with others. In just a couple of weeks the almost empty barn became a busy working barn as the trainer, Joe, moved in with several clients and their horses. The horses were mostly Quarter Horses and Joe was a western trainer. Among his clients was a lady, Paula Lynch. Her daughter, Deanna, and Jill soon became friends. I was so happy. I saw smiles on my daughter's face that had been absent for a long time. Even though she had decided to quit school, I felt if she could develop her natural talent with the horses she could survive.

September 2003 had arrived. I had met my landlady, Lynn, through the Cornell Cooperative Extension Service programs. They called and invited me to bring my Vanners to participate in "Open House on the Farm" to be held at the Thomas Bull Memorial Park. It would be a fun experience to spend the day at the park with Bandit and Magic and introduce people to the Gypsy Vanner Horse. Joe had a large trailer and was happy to transport the horses and my cart over to the park. We set up and prepared to do a demonstration. I drove Bandit and Jill rode Magic performing a few tricks with her center ring. The Cornell Extension Educator, Carrie Swanson, loved the horses and was thrilled when I offered to let her drive Bandit once around the ring.

We finished the demo and returned to the barn area. As I was removing Bandit's harness a lady with a slight accent came over to say hello. During the demo she had heard I was currently working at West Point and she wanted to let me know her husband was assigned there. She was originally from Sweden and had seen the interest in the Tinker horses, as she called them, growing in Europe before she left. I smiled realizing that over time I would help her to understand the difference in the gypsy horse population, and help her not only appreciate but understand the importance of the name Gypsy Vanner Horse. She was Linda Stewart, a dressage trainer and had worked at the upper levels of the discipline in Sweden. Even so, what she wanted was to learn to drive! And I wanted for my horses to be at least exposed to dressage to see if they could indeed perform in that discipline. However, with my current financial difficulties I had put that plan on hold. Linda made me an offer I simply could not refuse. She asked if I would give her driving lessons in return for dressage lessons! How could I say no? Once again as fate would have it another magical opportunity had come along for me and my horses that had woven their way into my life and truly changed its course.

A few days later back at the farm everyone was talking about taking horses to the Woodstock Riding Club Show. They were all practicing and preparing. Paula and Deanna suggested we think about bringing Bandit and Magic. Paula had heard they were offering driving classes. However, with everyone planning to go I didn't think there would be room for us. The day was getting closer and Joe said he thought he could fit us in as well as my cart.

Without really knowing what to expect we all loaded up the trailer and cars and were off for a show day at Woodstock. We entered Jill and Magic in the "Walk, Trot, Canter" English riding class and I entered Bandit in the three Driving Classes. All members of our barn family were warming up their horses while being coached by Joe from the side. Jill was on Magic looking lovely and it was just fun for me to watch as people would do a double take, wondering what kind of horse that was, or was that really a Gypsy Vanner here at Woodstock?

I prepared Bandit and the cart. Finally we were ready to drive over to the ring. Now, you have to understand that this driving thing was not well appreciated by the western barn family of which we had become a part, oh no indeed. There were snickers and wry grins as I prepared to head to the ring.

Standing at the ring gate was a man and woman who offered to open it for me. I thanked them as the woman questioned, "Is that one of those gypsies?" I proudly said, "This is a Gypsy Vanner". She then replied, "Wow, this one is really clean." This would be a comment I would remember. One I would later use to help explain how important presentation is, not just for a one time in the ring but for the breed and registry as well. In the northeast there had been owners of gypsy bred horses who brought them to Equine Affaire in Massachusetts or other local events giving little care to their cleanliness or their performance preparedness leaving in the minds of onlookers a less than acceptable view of these horses from gypsies.

Here we were, my boy and me, at our second show and I felt the smile on my face in spite of the drizzle of rain that was attempting to dampen the moment. I heard the judge asking us to trot and I urged Bandit into this with ease. I loved driving this horse! We followed the judge's directions walking, trotting, performing the working trot and finally lining up facing the judge. Davey, Joe's brother, worked as a handyman around the farm. He wasn't a horseperson and as a result felt left out of many activities. No matter everyone liked him and on this day I had a special job for him. I asked him to be my header for the day. This seemed to give him purpose and I was happy he wanted to help. As I brought Bandit to a stop Davey came running over and stood proudly in front of us.

The announcer began with first place and to my delight and surprise we had won the Pleasure Driving Class. Davey beamed as the ring steward handed him our blue ribbon. We competed in two additional driving classes taking third in each of those.

Driving Bandit at Woodstock Riding Club

After the driving classes I took care of Bandit putting him in a stall with hay and water and letting him have a much deserved rest while I went to find Jill. She was about to enter the ring on Magic for her class. They looked beautiful, but all the entries were dressed in beige breeches and blue jackets. I would learn later this was the expected attire for the class. Jill was dressed in black breeches and a black jacket. I thought she looked beautiful but this was not the appropriate dress and she and Magic did not place. Though they had performed quite well it was her dress and brightly colored saddle pad that stood in their way.

I felt terrible as I knew a ribbon would have meant far more to her than it did to me. We had scurried to the tack shop to find something for her to wear just days before the show. Never having competed in English riding classes we did not know the color of one's breeches was so important. Also, we had purchased a lovely purple edged in gold dressage saddle pad which was beautiful on Magic. This though was not the regulation pad for this class. These were lessons learned too late. I knew Jill wanted to place; she wanted to win, that was her nature. Suddenly, not her skill but rather what she was wearing had interfered with her success – she was disappointed. So was I.

Even so we realized it had been a really fun day. We all laughed, celebrated the wins, and just the enjoyment of the day as a whole.

After the Ohio EA Jacki Clark and I frequently telephoned each other sharing our horse stories, joys and troubles. We both were very concerned for Dennis Thompson and the future of the Gypsy Vanner Horse Society. Jacki was grateful to have Lash and she wanted to help in any way she could. She had reserved a booth at Massachusetts Equine Affaire in November 2003 for her business, Shirecrest Equine Education Center, of which she hoped Lash's Lessons would eventually be part. Jacki had kindly offered to share her booth with the Gypsy Vanner Horse Society. She wasn't sure if Dennis was going to be able to come or bring horses. She had therefore invited me to come and represent the GVHS and bring

Bandit. I began to have conversations with Deb Putnam of Equine Affaire and Becky Glover of the Gypsy Cob and Drum Horse Association. Both the GVHS and the GCDHA wanted to do demonstrations during the event, but EA had only allotted fifteen minutes for all the gypsy bred horses, no matter the registry. I felt the demonstrations should be separate. The GVHS promoted a single breed which did not allow crosses. The GCDHA represented not only Cobs but Drums which are crosses. To a person seeing these horses for the first time, a beautiful Drum, can be deceiving and appears the "same" as the breed horse. I therefore kindly asked that we divide the fifteen minutes between the two registries. I appreciated Becky's willingness to go along with my request.

Once it was determined that the GVHS would have a separate demonstration I began to work on a script and to see if I could find other Vanners to participate. Dennis did decide he could come and was bringing to my delight, The Gypsy King. Lynn Palm had been training King and I wanted to have her ride him as part of the demonstration and I would drive Bandit. With only days before the event I received an email from Dennis to tell me that Bill and Wendy Ricci would be there with their colt, Tinker Toy, who was in training with Phil Rogers. They wanted the colt to be included in the demo.

I emailed Phil Rogers and the Ricci's to see what Toy could do. I learned he was being tricked trained. With that I planned a demo that would begin with Lynn Palm riding The Gypsy King, followed by me driving Bandit while Tinker Toy under the direction of trainer, Phil Rogers, performed tricks in center ring.

The script and demo plan was approved by Deb Putnam and we were ready for Massachusetts Equine Affaire 2003. Once again, Joe was kind enough to trailer Bandit and all our accessories to West Springfield. We had reserved three stalls for The Gypsy King, Bandit and a tack stall between them. Toy was stalled in the Horse and Farm barn.

We set up the tack stall with a cot as Jill had said she would spend the night there to keep an eye on the horses.

Jacki and her daughter, Stacy, had beautifully decorated the booth. Once the booth was prepared, Jacki and I sat together to talk about the scheduling of horses for the booth stall. We felt that The Gypsy King should have prime time as he was the horse people knew and would want to see. Therefore, we thought it best to schedule him during the high traffic time or from late morning through early afternoon. I volunteered to have Bandit open the day as I knew Jill would already be there in the morning and of course I would arrive early each day to help her. This left the end of the day slot for Tinker Toy.

Wednesday night was cold, actually very cold and when I returned early Thursday morning I found a frozen Jill covered completely with human and horse blankets. I told her that as soon as we got the horses cared for and Bandit to the booth I would take her to the hotel where she could have a warm shower and sleep. She welcomed that idea.

I went over to Bill's (The Gypsy King's original name) stall to say hello. I was so happy that he was here; this was important; he is a credit to the breed. It was this horse pictured rearing in a crystal ball on the opening page of the Gypsy Gold website that had made me realize someone else understood. Someone else knew a breed did exist amongst a varied population of gypsy bred horses. I asked Jill if Dennis had been by and she had not seen him that morning. Since we were feeding Bandit we gave Bill some hay as well. We took Bandit out and groomed him in preparation for his debut in the booth.

Dennis still had not arrived. Jill brushed Bill and combed out that mass of feather with admiration. We felt we should at least do this just in case Dennis expected Bill to be first in the booth. Stacy came over via golf cart and said we needed to get the horse over as soon as possible since it was getting close to 8:45.

As planned Jill and I lead Bandit over and happily got him settled. Jacki had not seen Dennis either and we were getting a little concerned. At 9:00 the doors opened and Mass EA 2003 was officially underway. Shortly after the opening we heard a commotion over by the horse

75

entrance located near Deb Putnam's office. Then we saw Deb headed our way. She asked if we could help as Mr. Thompson was outside with his horse and wanted in. I said I would go and speak with him. I greeted Dennis and began to explain the schedule only to hear words I care not to repeat. I turned to Deb and asked for permission to switch Bandit and The Gypsy King. Wanting peace to return she begrudgingly agreed. Jill and I lead Bandit back to the stall area and I then took her to the hotel for the warmth and rest she needed.

When I returned I learned Jacki had a heart to heart with Dennis and starting the next morning the original schedule would be in place for the remainder of the event. I was relieved, but deep down what I really wanted was for Dennis to understand and accept the fact that Bandit and Tinker Toy were excellent breed examples and deserved the right to not only bear the name Gypsy Vanner Horse, but to proudly represent it.

I was quickly learning about the ups and downs of the equine world; the vying for position, the personalities; realizing the breed holding my heart was no different from any other. The trials and tribulations all breeds endure and overcome were just beginning for this rare and special treasure from the Gypsies.

We were all a little anxious as the time drew near for our demo. Bandit had been up the night before. Jill and I had driven him around while he pranced and showed us behaviors long forgotten. I trotted him back and forth to get him to settle down, but even then he was in a hurry as we started back to the barn, and we lost a favorite blanket as it blew out of the cart. When we returned after getting Bandit settled in his stall the blanket was nowhere to be found. Remembering this I was a bit nervous as I got him ready and hitched. However, this was a new day and he was back to being my old reliable Bandy boy that I so loved to drive. We headed over to the arena area and I drove him up and back a bit to warm him up and to calm my fears. Lynn arrived all beautifully dressed in a gypsy style vest making The Gypsy King appear even more regal. I stopped Bandit near the entrance and watched with pleasure these two perform. As Lynn exited, I drove Bandit into the arena, he quickened his pace but did as I asked while cameras flashed, Phil had followed with Tinker Toy and as I rounded the corner one last time I saw Toy taking a bow.

This was a very emotional moment for me – three beautiful breed horses had just paid tribute to the dedicated gypsy breeders who brought them to life and to a lady, Cindy Thompson, who had recognized the uniqueness of a little stallion running in a field in Wales. I was both pleased and proud as I invited Jacki to join me in the cart for the ride back to the barn area.

We would close out Massachusetts Equine Affaire 2003 with a sense of satisfaction for the Gypsy Vanner Horse Society. Yet, the variety of groups, individuals and gypsy bred horses attending had not improved the introduction of the breed to the United States. Dirty, unruly horses and mixed messages would continue to stay in my mind long after. To maintain my personal sanity with regards to the breed my focus would have to be on the horse, not the people.

During the summer of 2003 Jan Anderson and Lise McNamara imported a group of horses from Robert Watson in England. Among them were two colts. Lise was evaluating them for a possible future stallion for her breeding program. She chose the larger of the two and named him Blarney Stone's Sailor. His barn name was Blarney. The other colt had caught my eye. He was small as was his dam. While in Germany I had seen a twelve hand stallion on the cover of a publication for the Irish Cobs. He was beautiful and being that horses had come into my life after my prime, well the smaller and more manageable they were the better. If indeed I was ever to have a stallion in my life he would have to be a smaller one.

Lise's little colt had a sweet eye and I loved his markings. His name was Babes. Robert Watson had named him. Lise had purchased the mare in foal, but a delay in quarantine lead to the mare foaling while still in England. Robert had asked to keep the colt, but Lise had made the purchase and so the colt came with his dam to America.

On visits to Blarney Stone the colt truly endeared himself to me. At this time in my life having another horse seemed out of the question. I was continuing to work through the financial stresses of the last move and the remaining debt from our time in Port Jervis. I let Lise know that if I had the money this one would be coming home with me. Nonetheless someone did have the money and Babes was sold and sent to his new home in New Mexico.

While I could not have him, he had rekindled the hope of a little stallion. Someday, I thought, when times are better, I'll look for a Babes. Blarney Stone had become a place of peace for me as Lise and I became good friends sharing a genuine love of these horses. Being a mother of two sons and a daughter she understood my concerns with Jill. If Jill wasn't going to school maybe she would enjoy working with the horses at Blarney Stone. Lise and I made a plan, Jill would go down on Sunday afternoons, stay throughout the week and I'd pick her up and bring her home on the weekends. The months Jill spent at Blarney Stone were good ones. She enjoyed the farm and horses, but even more so the McNamara family.

Once again for a brief moment life was good. Linda Stewart and I had started working with Magic in dressage and driving Bandit. We planned our training sessions around Joe's schedule. Sunday evenings worked best. Linda was so impressed with the intelligence of the horses. She couldn't get over how quickly Magic understood and responded to her cues. I too was becoming more and more fascinated at my horses' ability to do so many different things.

As spring approached, Jacki Clark and I began to make plans for Ohio Equine Affaire 2004. Again, Jacki had reserved booth space not only for Shirecrest but also for the Gypsy Vanner Horse Society. This time in grand scale, she had a double booth with stalls as bookends.

Her "Lash's Lessons" program plans were progressing; character prototypes had been designed and the first book was being finalized. Jacki and I spent many hours on the phone discussing the wonderful possibilities for this program and how it would benefit America's children while honoring the breed. For two little old lady school teachers, the realization of this program would be a dream come true.

Dennis did not plan on attending Equine Affaire. Jacki and Stacy were bringing Lash and they invited me to bring Magic as our focus would be on the breed's incredible temperament. Magic was not the horse I took to exemplify the breed – for that it was Bandit, who is without a doubt the epitome of what a gypsy's vision horse should be. My girl on the other hand had a larger head than I liked, a little longer back, yet her temperament and intelligence astounded everyone who met her. Her mane, tail and feathering were lovely. I like her pattern, the black is well defined on the white; black head with white blaze complimented by an all white mane gives her the look that deserves her name. I frequently tell people she is the most intelligent animal I have ever owned; I would not be surprised if one morning she greeted me in plain English rather than her normal welcoming whinny.

Jacki and I had discussed what we should do for the GVHS demo since once again the demo for gypsy bred horses would be equally divided between the GVHS and the Gypsy Cob and Drum Horse Association. Brenda Moore had contacted me asking if she might bring her Grand Vanner stallion, Ard Ri, to participate in the demo. Her young daughter would ride him. We had an eight year old girl, Nicole, who had been enjoying riding Magic just for fun yet under Jill's skillful hand. Nicole took riding lessons with Joe at our barn. As I began to plan the demo I thought it would be most appropriate to have Nicole ride Magic to demonstrate the quiet, manageability of the breed, and for the stallion, Ard Ri to be ridden as well by a young girl would certainly attest to this trait.

This Equine Affaire was somewhat more stressful than the previous. Things were getting a little complicated at our barn and this trip brought some of those problems along for the ride. The GVHS was undergoing difficulties. I felt Jacki and I were doing our best to keep it afloat, but felt somewhat unappreciated and alone. Gypsy Gold was still struggling and trying to overcome Cindy's loss. The Gypsy Vanner Horse Society had just started to take off as a registry with Cindy doing most of the necessary paperwork. With her death, things got lost and in some instances we had to go back to square one. The other gypsy bred horse organizations without these difficulties to contend with began to grow. For someone who truly appreciated the Thompson's work and foundational beginnings for this breed, I was frustrated and exhausted.

Jill was not happy on this trip. I was becoming more and more concerned about her feelings and outlook. She was sad often and when she was she shut down and wouldn't talk. I don't know how she got things so confused in her head about our demo, but she did. Somehow, she thought she was supposed to ride Magic during the demo, yet for weeks we had been practicing with Nicole. The day of the demo arrived and I was watching the clock and had asked her to help get Magic ready with Nicole. We were almost late and while we were waiting at the entrance to the arena she began to argue that she was to ride Magic.

I tried to explain, she was to stand center ring for safety, but Nicole would be the rider. Sharp words passed between us. She was angry and almost refused to enter the ring. Nicole rode Magic and though Magic spooked a little Nicole managed to keep her on course and complete the demo ride.

Our little group from the Walden farm, Jill's irritability, and supporting a struggling GVHS was creating much stress for me at this event. If that wasn't enough, Deb Putnam stopped by to say that Dennis had arrived, with no horses, even though he had made stall reservations. He had scheduled the use of her office for a GVHS meeting. At 2:00 on March 25, 2004 fifteen GVHS members crowded into the small space made available to us by Deb P. Anxiety was high; Cindy's death,

Dennis' uncertainties regarding how to manage the registry, and lack of communication on many issues brought members in search of answers. My greatest disappointment was his unwillingness to allow Jacki Clark to get the GVHS organized and properly set up as a 501c(3). So, I was one of fifteen members who came to hear, but also to help. Dennis presided and the minutes of that meeting are available for those who wish to read them. Basically they share that a new partnership had been formed between Dennis Thompson and Doug Kneis, a Texas businessman. Mr. Kneis had his lawyer, Thomas Kinnerly draw up the necessary documents to make the GVHS officially a Texas nonprofit organization as of 25 March, 2004. Dennis Thompson would serve as the GVHS President while Mr. Kneis would be Vice President. Barbara Snyder was introduced as the Treasurer and was coming to the organization with past experience as a VP for an international manufacturing company.

The meeting minutes record discussions on breeding issues, private business endeavors, a new website, newsletter, forms, and the establishment of working committees; in other words the beginning work of a fledgling organization. My contribution was to serve as the newsletter editor, but I left the meeting feeling ill. I was not happy with the way things had been done.

I had met Doug K. at the 2003 meeting in Ohio. He was definitely a businessman with a focus on the bottom line. Don't misunderstand – I have no problem with anyone making a profit and I do hope over time that many farms are successful with this breed. Doug's partnering with Dennis had the potential for good. However, large scale importing and selling of horses had already begun to be detrimental to this breed and I feared this partnership was headed in that direction. While it could be profitable for both gentlemen, it did not seem designed for the good of the whole – the GVHS and the breed.

After Dennis introduced him, Doug took the floor and Dennis was reduced to sitting while Doug directed the remainder of the meeting.

I watched Dennis' face and felt so sorry for him. The GVHS was now officially a nonprofit breed registry, yes, but at what cost? This meeting left me feeling that business rather than this incredible breed would be the driving force. When I returned to the booth, Jacki noticed I was visibly shaken. When she asked if I was alright, I broke into tears.

The remaining days somehow passed but the peace was missing on this trip. Magic, however, was the best possible example for the Vanner temperament. She allowed the touching and petting of hundreds of visitors and never once showed any sign of disapproval, in fact she was so good Dr. Groom asked if he could use her as his model for several of his presentations.

Dr. Groom explains his products with our Magic being his model.

We returned home to the routine and rhythm of our daily lives. Jill continued working at Blarney Stone; and life went on. Over time I felt less comfort in this barn and on this farm. Joe's group dominated everything, I was beginning to feel most unwelcome, yet this was my home first. My paddock for Magic and Bandit had been overtaken and I was told I would have to share it. Storage had forced my cart to be moved outside with a tarp to cover it. Driving was definitely not the discipline of choice by the majority of the occupants. In fact I was made to feel "in the way". Linda Stewart and I continued our work with Magic and Bandit, however it wasn't easy. It would be our time to use the arena and, one of Joe's families started to make it a point to be in the arena and not show any sign of leaving even though it was our scheduled time. Linda was a true professional and would kindly ask how long they planned to be. They would say a few minutes and stay longer. After this happened a few times Linda was upset as she could see this was intentional.

In spite of obvious obstacles Linda and I continued our weekly sessions until her husband received orders to return to Germany. I believe Linda was happy to be able to return to Europe. We had such fun for the few months we worked together with my horses. Magic had shown promise with dressage and Linda had been introduced to driving. We had accomplished, maybe not all we hoped for, but certainly we learned and had fun. Spring had arrived.

One evening I got a call from Dennis. The summer of 2003 we had tried several times to breed Magic to Gypsy Gold's Roadsweeper. I had so admired this stallion at the Ohio Equine Affaire 2003, Dennis had said my mare could have his first foal. We tried all summer and when it did not work in August, I explained we might try the following spring. I did not want a foal on the ground this late in the year in New York. Now spring was back and Dennis wanted to know if I was ready to try again to breed Magic to Roadsweeper. I said indeed I did. He explained in order to breed to Sweeper I would have to send Magic to Florida. Loss of semen motility in transport had been the reason we had not been able to successfully get Magic in foal the previous summer. While sending the mare to Florida might have been an option for most people, the expense of such an undertaking would not be something I could afford. I kindly had to explain this would not work for me.

I thanked Dennis for everything and said I'd try and find a stallion close by for my girl or wait until I could send her to Florida. I was fine with that. However, a few days later Dennis called back. He was disappointed things had not worked out with the breeding and so he offered me a dream come true – a breeding to my choice of his other stallions as an exchange for the Sweeper breeding that had not worked!

I could not believe it! He did not have to hear me say the stallion's name, he knew. He simply said, "Let me know when I need to get Bok collected." I told him I'd have my vet out the very next day to check Magic.

I called the vet first thing after getting to my office the next day. I figured they would check her and then let me know about how long I'd have to wait to get this underway. Wrong! About eleven o'clock the vet called to ask how quickly we could get semen here. I explained I didn't know but I'd call the stallion owner immediately. I finally found Dennis in route to Texas, but he said he would call the repro folks and they would be in touch with me. They called to say that semen was being put on a plane to Newark International Airport and should arrive around 11:00 that evening. Once I knew this I called the vet, who said to give her a call once we had the semen at the farm.

I hurried home from work, Jill, Davey the handyman, and I started on our drive to Newark, NJ. Newark International at that time was not the easiest airport to navigate. I stopped more than once to ask how to get to the cargo area. No one I asked seemed to know, when I was about ready to scream I saw a man pushing a custodial cart, and he kindly gave me the directions. Time was running out as I pulled up to the cargo office. Two gentlemen were standing behind the desk and I guess they could see how anxious I was as one greeted me saying, "You must be here to pick up the baby in a bottle".

Once we had the precious blue equitainer in hand off we sped back to the farm. It was a lovely night, the moon was full and there wasn't a cloud in the sky. As I was driving up the driveway I excitedly called my vet. She said she was on the way. I stood in front of the barn looking up at the beautiful moon as the vet's truck came to a stop. As she opened the truck door, I excitedly said hello. To which she responded, "Joyce, no one should be this happy this time of night." We both laughed. Magic calmly allowed the process to take place; it was old hat since we had done this so many times the year before. The deed was done and the vet was gone. I looked quietly at the beautiful night sky one more time before climbing the stairs to the apartment.

The few weeks of waiting passed and Sandy the repro vet arrived on a busy Saturday morning at the farm to check Magic. As the vet truck pulled up in front of the barn folks started to gather wanting to know who was sick. I was taking Magic out of the stall and calmly said that no one was sick, she was just going to check Magic. Once the ultra sound machine was set up Sandy began the scan. I was holding Magic and then as the vet had done so many times the previous summer, she asked me to come back and look at the screen. Someone held Magic while I went back to look. Every time before the sad news had been it didn't take. This time as Sandy moved over the screen there was a small bleep. She asked, "Did you see that?" "Yes," I said. "Let me do that again", was her reply. As it passed once again a small bleep was heard and this time Sandy said, "That is your first look at your baby."

Both Sandy and I were giggling with pleasure. I could not have been happier. Magic was in foal to Cushti Bok! The horse that had started it all for the Thompsons, was America's first, and for me had confirmed that my suspicions of a true breeding program by gypsies did indeed exist.

While we were happy, others occupying the barn were not. This to them was a boarding barn and now my mare was in foal. Even after explaining that Lynn knew my plans for breeding Magic and even if possible to acquire a stallion, they still found this hard to swallow.

Somehow, I could not get a grip on my feelings or understand theirs. I had moved to the apartment and began boarding my horses here;

outlining clearly with my landlady my hopes and plans with my horses before any of these people arrived. Now, how they felt and what they wanted appeared to be taking precedent over my prior arrangements.

For the moment I decided not to worry and try to focus on being happy and taking special care of my girl during this time. It was indeed a grand way for me to begin my summer. Shortly after Magic was confirmed in foal, Lise called sharing a dilemma. Seems Merrow's owner had decided she didn't want this young stallion. She wasn't prepared to handle a stallion; so per contract Lise was to have first option of buying him back. Alone this would not have been problematic, but Lise had also received a message from Babes' owner in New Mexico. Due to a family health issue Babes too would be returning to Blarney Stone.

With Blarney this would be three stud colts on the property and Lise did not see how this was going to work. She asked me if I was still interested in Babes. Of course I was, but I was continuing to function on limited finances. However, because of the situation, friendship, and knowing he would be loved and cared for she offered to let me have him through a payment plan.

I thought of Jacki Clark's program with Lash, Merrow's half brother, and hoped Jacki might be interested in the colt. I called Jacki and put her in touch with Lise. Soon afterwards Merrow found himself on the way to Kentucky to become involved with all the programs at Shirecrest. With Merrow going to Jacki and Babes coming to me we had solved Lise's dilemma and found forever homes for both colts.

I approached my landlady regarding Babes and his arrival. I offered to repair the paddock in back of the barn and use the run in as a stall. She was happy to have the area cleaned and repaired. Now that I had found my stud colt I was pleased that Lynn was honoring her agreement to allow him to join me at the Walden farm.

Joe's boarders were not pleased. Two mare owners wanted assurance the paddock would have electric fence. I made certain of that while explaining this little guy was nothing to dread.

The day Lise delivered Babes a couple of boarders were on hand to witness the arrival of the "big, bad stud", only to see tiny, fluffy Babes back off the trailer. He was small. It was my hope he would remain small, after all I wanted a "little stallion". To have this horse in my life was nothing less than magical.

Onlookers present at his arrival laughed at the unwarranted fears of those believing anyone would be at risk because of this colt. Each afternoon I'd walk him down the quarter mile driveway to the mailbox. Often I would hear a snicker, as someone would say as we passed, "There goes Joyce and her big, bad stallion!" Those walks were great for me and for him. A partnership began there.

Lise's friend, Kathy who did the beginning basic groundwork with her foals had trained Babes to lunge. He was so small I could lunge him on a lead line. This being another activity which caused giggles from fellow boarders. He was the sweetest of colts and I was having great fun with him.

My life continued its roller coaster pattern – good times interrupted abruptly by bad (sometimes very bad) times. Jill left Blarney Stone over night. Going to live with a man she had met and hardly knew. Yet, I believe Lise was ready for her to leave. Attitude and defiance minus gratitude would make anyone unwelcome – this too was beginning to become a pattern.

What she left behind was more than a job and a place to live. A horse had come into her life through Jan Anderson. A beautiful gelding named, Lir. He originally was purchased by a woman in NJ who called a short while after he arrived to say the horse appeared unsound. Lise agreed to bring the horse back to Blarney Stone and have the vet examine him again. It was determined that he had arthritis in both hocks due to pulling a heavy gypsy wagon for years. Since the woman no longer wanted him given this condition, Jan decided to offer him to Jill as Lise had shared with her the special relationship between this horse and girl.

Lise decided to put a price on the horse as she felt Jill should earn him. She explained Jill could work off the price. Lir adored Jill and the feeling was apparently mutual. Believing one day Lir would live with us we brought him to the farm in Walden for the weekend. We had scheduled a photo shoot with a young photographer.

Jill with Lir

This was and continues to be my favorite photograph of Jill and the horses. No matter how many times she has been photographed with all the others, she never exudes the love I see here.

Nonetheless she left with the boyfriend leaving Lir behind. Had I been financially stable and had the money I would have gladly claimed him. Yet, to figure out how to pay and care for another horse at that time was not possible. Lise took ownership since Jill had not worked off the price required.

Eventually Lise donated Lir to Jacki Clark's program and he joined Merrow in Kentucky. I was happy for him to go there as I knew he would have a wonderful home. Jill's poor choices and unfortunate circumstances had cost her something special. She and Lir had developed a wonderful relationship – true partners. Even though he was in a good home and safe I felt he certainly could not understand why Jill had deserted him. Jill would later blame Lise and me for Lir not being in her life. I hurt again for my daughter and her inability to see or grasp reality.

The winds of change were blowing at Heritage Farm in autumn 2004. Joe and friends had been slowly making needed improvements to the place; new wall boards in the indoor; painting; fences repaired and finally a load of beach sand footing for the indoor arrived.

When I mentioned all this activity to my landlady she indicated Joe might buy the property. I felt this would be a good thing for Joe and also for Lynn, knowing she had wanted to sell the farm for some time. Regardless such an arrangement would not work in my favor. Joe and I tolerated each other. He saw no value in my chosen breed or in my chosen discipline of driving. It was becoming clear another move was on the horizon for me and my precious horses. It would not be easy this time with a stud colt and mare in foal. Your average boarding stable would not allow this. I found myself once again in search of a miracle.

One night I received a phone call making me forget my troubles at least for a brief moment. When I answered the phone I heard something I had begun to miss, a lovely southern accent. I smiled as a lady named Carliss Henderson asked if she could buy my Bandit. While times for me since coming to New York had been hard Bandit simply was not for sale. Carliss seemed quite disappointed. She shared she was recovering from a life threatening stroke. Her physical therapist had asked if she liked horses. No, she did not like horses, she loved horses!

However, raising five children and holding down a full time job had left little time for anything else. She had taken her therapist's advice and purchased a miniature horse mare. After a few months of playing with this horse Carliss' balance improved remarkably. It was such a change for the better her therapist suggested she might want to consider a full size horse. Carliss' husband, Jerry, happy to have his wife healthy once more told her she could have any horse she wanted. That promise sent her to the internet where she found Bandit. While I could not offer her Bandit, I knew Jan Anderson had a new colt; all black with four white feet and a white blaze. I asked Carliss if she might be interested. I called Jan and put her in touch with Carliss. Soon after I received two phone calls one from an excited Carliss who had purchased the colt and named him Curaco. The second from Jan thanking me for helping her find such a wonderful home for the colt.

I enjoyed the brief moment of joy, and then returned to my daunting reality. By December I was quite unhappy. It was public knowledge Joe was buying the Walden farm. He was setting up his rules.

A letter had been given to all boarders of the increased prices effective 1 February. The indoor with its beach sand (way too much I might add) was unusable for me. I refused to work my horses in that much sand. I had been looking for other places and due to a stud colt and pregnant mare I was not having much luck.

It was winter; no one moves in winter in New York. All my horsey friends were doing their best to make inquiries in search of a new home for me and my menagerie. While we might find an apartment willing to accept the dog and cats there would be no barn close by. I finally found a barn that would take my horses: stud colt, gelding, and pregnant mare. It was Journey's End farm. The owner, Jenny, was delightful and seemed to appreciate my current woes and genuinely wanted to help. She and

I both were busy searching for rentals in the area which would allow my pets. Finally Jenny called to say she had found an apartment about a mile from her farm. We had scheduled an appointment to see it on a Sunday afternoon in mid January 2005.

Shortly before my daughter, Jamie, arrived to pick me up to go and see the apartment my phone rang. It was Sherry Cashman, she had just been in our favorite tack store, *Whinnies and Knickers*. Sherry mentioned all my difficulties to Kathy, the store clerk. To which Kathy smiled and pulled a small piece of paper from beside the computer.

As she handed it to Sherry she said, "This just came in this morning. Tell Joyce to call right away." The people were offering a small house and a four stall barn! I thanked Sherry and quickly dialed the number.

A woman answered. I shared I worked at West Point and was interested in the house and the barn. With a slight pause and a deep breath I continued, "I have a mare in foal with a due date in May. I also have a stud colt turning two in April, and my gelding."

There was no change in her voice as she said, "Sure, no problem." So I went on, "I also have a dog and two cats." To which she responded, "We love animals here, so we will see you this afternoon?" As I hung up the phone I was momentarily frozen in time; this couldn't possibly be happening. It was simply too perfect. I snapped out of it as I heard Jamie's car pull up to the barn.

We drove out to the apartment near Journey's End. When I had first found Jenny's farm I thought its name suggested what I was looking for; but as Jamie and I pulled up to the apartment house I realized this wasn't what we needed. The house set only a few feet from the highway. Though out in the country it was busy enough to be a risk for my dog and cats should one get out. Steep stairs and very tiny rooms with limited storage made it clear this was not for us.

Once back in the car I directed Jamie to go north on Route 9W to Marlboro. It seemed as if we had been driving for quite a while when we finally saw the "Welcome to Marlboro" sign. We decided it was a drive but certainly not anything like the drive to and from Port Jervis. The directions said to make a left onto Mt. Rose Road. We followed the steep hill up and around to the very top where we were to meet the woman at the barn. January's ice and snow covered the ground, but the road was clear. We saw the barn and pulled in.

The young woman was all smiles as she showed us the perfect four stall barn with tack room, wash stall, and hayloft. Looking around I thought my horses would be so happy and comfortable here. She then directed us to the indoor which was twice the size of the one in Walden; there was no excess beach sand here. My heart smiled. She suggested we all get in her truck and drive down to the little house. It was a cottage; the kitchen had been recently renovated and was charming. A tiny dining room spilled into the living room. All rooms had plenty of windows letting in the late afternoon sun. Upstairs were two bedrooms and a full bath. Again I felt I had been given another chance to keep my dream alive. It was just right, as Goldilocks would say.

As we returned to the barn I was calculating what this was going to cost and with those thoughts the dream was fading. Once at the barn the young woman, now known as Tara invited us to walk over to her father's house.

She explained I would be renting the house from her and the barn from her father. As we walked she pointed out the tennis court to our right and the swimming pool to our left saying these could be used by the tenants. We entered the back door of the main house and found ourselves in a beautiful den with a warm fire going in the large fireplace. Tara introduced us to her father, Peter Lordi, a distinguished looking gentleman who welcomed us and invited us to have a seat.

As Tara shared our interests her father nodded. Finally I reiterated we certainly would enjoy the opportunity to live on this lovely property with all of our animals. Unfortunately, I was operating on a very tight budget and felt more than likely this would not be a place I could presently afford. At which Mr. Lordi inquired as to what I was currently paying. He looked at Tara and she returned his glance; then he stated a price for the house and barn that was only $100 more a month than what I was presently paying! We thanked Tara and Peter making arrangements to move in on February 1, 2005.

Now, this was not just a fairytale moment, I felt it was divine intervention, and uncontrollable tears flowed. The warmth of the fire on this cold January afternoon, and the warm welcome and gift of everything I needed and more was simply a revelation that God is good and He was most certainly taking care of me.

To be honest I have always been amazed how often and how clearly God has intervened in my life. I certainly have not been the best of His children. When my second daughter was born I was at a low point. A wonderful devout Catholic friend, Becky Singer was concerned for me. She came to visit shortly after the birth. Prayer being an integral part of her day, she wanted to encourage me to remember to talk with God. If I felt no one else would listen I could certainly trust Him to do so was her belief. To further get me started in this process, one that had been in my earlier years vital to me, she suggested we pray together.

A few days passed and Becky returned to see how mom and baby were doing. We had a nice visit and as she was starting to leave she said, "I have to tell you that I believe God wants me to give you a specific Bible verse. Each night since my last visit when I would began my personal devotion time you would come to mind as would this verse. If I tried to shake those thoughts and move on to my study you and this verse would seem to be stronger in my mind. I know I must give this verse to you. It is Jeremiah 29: 11. I thanked her and said good-bye. When I returned to my room I found my Bible and opened it to the verse:

"For I know the plans I have for you says the Lord; to prosper you and not harm you; to give you a future and a hope". – Jeremiah 29:11

As I read the words it was as if I could here a voice saying them. Deep inside I felt God was letting me know that my troubles were real, but his plans for me had not changed. I felt peaceful for the first time in months; I fell asleep next to my tiny daughter sleeping quietly in her beautiful German bassinet. Life moved on. About six months later I received a letter from a wonderful college roommate that I had not heard from in years. She had traced me down through my sister. Sharon was writing to tell me about her recent marriage, but this was not the only reason. In her letter she shared how attending Bible study had been enjoyed with her future husband during their dating days. Now in married life they continued with a family Bible time. She wanted me to know they had a favorite verse and recently whenever she would read the verse I would come to mind. This happened so frequently she felt it was important to find me and share the verse with me. That verse was Jeremiah 29:11.

Tears filled my eyes; I closed them and began to pray, "Dear God, I hear You. I don't know where we are going, but I know You have a plan for me. I have to trust You to get me there."

Of course this all happened years before my daughter and I drove up Mount Rose Road and found the little house and barn. Yet, those memories, "my verse", and God's plan for me was evident and staring me in the face as I realized how improbable it was to find this place at this time of year, within the time frame I needed. I was here because this was what I needed to stay within the plan. Again, I closed my eyes and thanked God for this most welcomed opportunity.

February 2005 found us settling in at the cottage on the Lordi estate. Three horses now called the little barn home; the fourth stall was occupied by two rabbits belonging to Tara. Before leaving for her home in Florida she had asked if I would take care of them. Happy to be here; happy to have this barn and my horses safe in it, taking care of two rabbits seemed a small request for what I felt I owed Tara and her father.

It was a pleasure getting to know all the people who shared this property and called it home. Some were like us, just passing through and yet others had planted roots.

The little barn was connected to a larger barn by a walkway and bell tower. Ed Calabrese rented that barn. He was a hunter-jumper trainer, well respected and acclaimed in the area. Horses came and went from his barn as they were trained.

However, he had one regular tenant, Barbara A., who owned a beautiful Thoroughbred gelding named Winston. Both Ed and Barbara were friendly and politely acknowledged my fluffy ponies. Now, let's be real, Gypsy Vanners certainly have the heart and can do attitude to take on the hunter-jumper world, but more than likely they will not. Ed and Barb were hard core in that world; time, energy, and dedication were there. It was clear as long as my Vanners did their thing and it did not conflict with the established jumping schedule then all would be right with the world. That worked for me.

There was such a sense of satisfaction and peace each morning when MacIntosh and I walked up the hill to the barn. No one else was there; no one else had horses there, just Bandit, Magic, and Babes.

The two rabbits did not have names; only a couple days after I arrived the older of the rabbits died. I felt sorry for the one left and began to spend more time with him. He had to have a name and he became Bugs.

My mornings were peaceful and enjoyed. My horses were such gifts; I loved each one dearly. They had different personalities which endeared them even more to me. Magic was growing bigger every day. Each morning with excitement and anticipation I took the stethoscope and listened to the baby. It was due in May.

Bandit was Mr. Grumpy. Not really, but he had this part of his personality, I believe left over from his stallion days, causing him to be independent appearing to be unapproachable. Yet, once in his stall the head came down, the soft manly whinny begged for a shoulder

rub while he began his morning hay. I loved this horse….a treasure…..
my one of a kind…..the rope on the porch had wanted and waited
for him.

Babes was growing up; the testosterone was kicking in; beautiful,
bold and pushy. I was beginning to feel maybe this was more than I
could handle; yet, I wanted this stallion. I wanted to honor through
Babes' foals Robert Watson and the other dedicated gypsy breeders
who had given this breed life; this young stallion and I would have to
grow together.

On some mornings I would be greeted by Patti on her way to the
dumpster by the barn. She lived in what I called the "gate house". The
property had two entrances; the one near the barn was the driveway
around Peter's house, the other came in by a small house divided into two
apartments. Patti lived in the front apartment and had been introduced
to me by Tara as the "cookie lady". That title soon became apparent as
Patti began to bring "goodies" by for me and the girls.

A wonderful cook she loved to entertain. A friendship formed
that was enjoyed by both of us. We had special dinners; went on
shopping outings; sipped homemade concocted drinks by the pool,
and laughed……and laughed…….and laughed. It was fun.

In the other gatehouse apartment lived Jim DeWitt and his fiancé
Jen. Jim was a handyman for the property; he made repairs, cut trees,
and ran the farm equipment when it was needed.

Across the street from the main house was a larger two story house
owned by Tara. Jay, an old beau of Tara's, now rented the house with
a couple of roommates. Tara and Jay had gotten together because of a
mutual love of polo. Jay still maintained a small polo herd; three to five
polo ponies were kept in pastures just below the paddocks occupied by
Ed's horses.

There was a small one bedroom apartment above the four stall
barn that now housed my horses. A young man by the name of Chris,
lived there.

Different people, different personalities and pursuits, all had come together on this beautiful hill overlooking the Hudson. I believe all of us found it to be a place of solace and needed to be here at this time in our lives.

All were excited about Magic's coming foal. Each seemed to take a personal interest in her care. When I left for school in the morning my worries were lessened as I knew Ed, Jay, Patti, Chris, Jim and Jen would stop in and check on Magic. They all reported to me each afternoon when I arrived. It was great!

In April Babes turned two years old. He had become a handful. My experience was limited and he knew it. Walking him down to the paddock for turn out was a battle. He pulled, reared, backed up, all with me on the other end of the lead. I reluctantly retrieved him from the paddock each afternoon, usually with an audience all with lots of advice, but no one ever came over to take the lead out of my hand. On one such warm spring afternoon, I went to the paddock opened the gate and was able to get the lead on Babes' halter with little difficulty, but then he charged the gate dragging me out with him. Yes, I knew it would be best to bring him back in and get him to wait and walk out with me. Not today, he was too strong, and I was not at a point to take that on just yet. As he pulled me toward the outdoor arena, Ed and Peter watched. I got control as we entered the arena and I began to turn him in circles. Both Ed and Peter began to give advice when all of a sudden Babes jumped forward and I could not hold him; he was free and ran into Jay's yard. Ed ran after and caught him. With the chain across his nose he backed him up what seemed like fifty yards! After which Babes walked back to the barn with me like a gentleman. Peter and Ed followed suggesting for the hundredth time that I should geld this horse.

My knees were weak as I turned him towards me in his stall and took off his halter. I looked into those fire filled yet soft brown eyes and knew that gelding was never an option, not with this horse.

Babes age 2 running in his paddock.
(Photo courtesy of Heidi Gridley)

The little cottage was home. It felt right, even though the cost of moving there had not been cheap. This was my ever present struggle. I could not seem to get a grip on the expense of living in NY. With all the moves there had been no relief time to catch up. Having truly never been in debt in my life this change was a difficult one to face. I always had more in savings or investments than my bills; now the reverse was becoming a dreadful truth. No matter my efforts to put aside and try and save there was always an unexpected five hundred dollar expense that somehow appeared. Credit cards were maxed out. When my pay check arrived it was spent. For the first time in my entire working life I felt poor.

The thought of selling a horse was ever present, but strongly avoided. My horses were my hope; my future. Maybe I could sell Magic's foal.

Now that Babes was my stallion, if the foal was a colt it would seem that I should sell it. From February until late May we settled in and enjoyed the anticipation of the foal's arrival.

Everyone was anxious as the time due near. I drove my vet, Dr. Eric Peterson, crazy with questions and calls. He finally told me that he was not coming out to check Magic again as she was fine and the foal was positioned properly. He did not want to keep having to charge me for a farm call when all was well. Truthfully the calls were more for me; to calm me; give me reassurance than for Magic. I loved this mare. I worried that something could happen. I wanted her and her baby to be well.

She was two weeks past her due date and I had begun to sleep on a cot in the barn aisle next to her stall. What was fascinating is that Bandit and Babes enjoyed having me spend the night with them. They looked out and checked on me from time to time and there was this incredible feeling of peace in this barn with my horses.

Each morning they woke me ready to be fed. I'd stretch and greet them as I threw back the blanket usually just as Ed's car pulled in at the barn next door. Now, he'd come over just to see if we had a baby. On Saturday morning I noticed that Magic seemed a little uncomfortable, but she began eating her hay as usual. I decided I would put her out with Bandit since I was home and could keep an eye on her.

She remained outside all day and when I brought the two of them in she seemed happy to find the quiet and rest her stall provided. I finished my barn chores and realized I was truly tired and worn out from all these nights on the cot. At about 9:00 I knocked on Chris' door and told him I was going to the house to get a few hours sleep in a real bed. I asked if he would call me if he heard any unusual sounds from Magic. He agreed he would.

I didn't undress; just fell across the bed and almost immediately was asleep. I was awakened by the phone at 11:00. It was Chris saying Magic was making funny sounds.

I quickly grabbed my flashlight and ran up the hill to the barn. As I entered I was doing my best to keep quiet so I would not frighten her. As I turned the light towards her I found her lying down and when she saw it was me she gently raised her tail so I could see the bag just beginning to appear.

Shaking I began dialing my vet's number; Chris had come down and I asked him to run and tell everyone that Magic was having her baby. To my relief Dr. Peterson was on call that night. I asked if he was on the way and he reassured me that before he could get there the baby would be born, so he was going to coach me through this. By now we had an audience; Chris was back with his girlfriend, Jessica. Jim and Jen were there and Patti arrived in her night gown. Dr. Peterson asked if I could see the feet. Yes, two little feet were poking out and they were in the right position pointing down. Shortly you should see the nose I heard him saying. I sat down and waited and sure enough with a push the nose and head appeared. Dr. Peterson said that Mother Nature would do the rest and he hung up. Another push and the baby rolled out and into my lap.

Someone handed me the towel from my foaling kit and I gently peeled back the sack and began to dry off this fine foal as it immediately tried to stand. Wobbly legs took their first step as Magic with gentle sounds and a soft nudge guided it to nurse. I got up and retrieved the bucket to hold the afterbirth. I had to walk around behind Magic for about a half hour until all the afterbirth was out. All the while the baby nursed and walked around Magic and me.

Everyone was thrilled and excited about being there for the birth. Most had expressed their congratulations and returned to their beds. I sat down again in the soft straw and watched this miracle. Morning came without me even realizing how long I had been there.

The foal was a colt; a son of Cushti Bok, America's first Gypsy Vanner Horse stallion. With this lineage Magic's colt was also a grandson of The Old Horse of Wales, one of my favorite foundation sires in the breed. I had hoped for a filly to breed to my Babes – combining The Old Horse of Wales line with the UK Roadsweeper line was something I hoped to do in my breeding program one day. The month of June was filled with visitors stopping by to see the new baby and to admire him. Coming up with a name had been a process. Initially Dennis and I had decided it should be a name that recognized both Magic and Bok.

Dennis had suggested "Cushti Bok's Magic Destiny". I liked the name and knew it would be a good one for either a filly or a colt. The night before the foal was born; Patti had invited me over for a light dinner. She knew I wasn't taking the time to cook for myself. While Patti and I were sitting on her patio having dinner Peter wandered over and sat down. His first question was, "Do we have a baby yet?" Of course he knew that if we had he would know as well as everyone on the hill.

He then asked if I had picked out a name for it. I told him I had. "You know," he said, "being the first Gypsy Vanner born in New York and from a breed originating in England maybe you should have the name reflect this historical place of birth. Marlboro gets its name from the Duke of Marlborough who lived in this area when England ruled."

After dinner and on my walk back over to the barn I had considered Peter's suggestion. Now that the foal was born I needed to make up my mind on a name. If I named him with history in mind it could not be for the Duke of Marlborough, Duke was a dog's name. Royalty though was what he was; a new breed; his sire truly the first in America; maybe Lord Marlborough I thought.

The more I said it the more I liked it. Many owners of foals by Cushti Bok had included his name in the foal's name and I liked that as well. I finally thought of Cushti Bok's Lord Marlborough. A mouthful for certain but a name worthy of this fine boy; however, saying that every time you called him could be a little much. A barn name was needed. Again I thought of just how much it had meant to me to have this barn and little house. How Peter and Tara had made it possible by not charging me an outlandish rent so that I could live here. To honor that support and goodness I decided on the barn name, "Lordi" for the colt. It was short for Lord Marlborough and it was the family name for Peter and Tara. That worked.

Cushti Bok's Lord Marlborough (Lordi) on an early outing with his dam, Magic. (Photo courtesy of Heidi Gridley)

Shortly after Lordi was born I decided to contact the Times Herald Record, our local newspaper. I wanted people to begin to know about and understand this breed and my little colt would make a good ambassador like his Uncle Bandit I thought. Happily I received a phone call back from the reporter, Deb Mendenbach. She scheduled a time to come out and see the horses and talk with me. Again I saw this breed work their magic on a person first encountering them. Within a matter of minutes she was hooked. Instead of spending just a short time, she spent a few hours with me. Her photographer snapped photos and as I answered her questions, more questions came. I was happy to have found a venue to share my personal experience with the horses but more so to celebrate not only their European history but their American beginnings – that is what Lordi encompassed.

As Deb left and thanked me for this special day she stated that she would let me know when the article would appear. When the call came it was to tell me her editor loved the story so much we would have a full page in the Sunday paper!

When I arrived at school on Monday I was met by colleagues who had seen the article and congratulated me. Several didn't even know I had horses in my life and they were fascinated with this side of me. I believe this was the time I began to celebrate and share what my horses meant to me with those at work who saw me as an administrator and their boss.

Near the end of the week after the article was in the paper I received a call from Lenny Miller. Mr. Miller was in charge of the "Salute to Agriculture" exhibit at the Dutchess County Fair held annually in Rhinebeck, NY. This fair is second in size only to the New York State Fair and has thousands of visitors. His wife had seen the article and thought Lordi and Magic might be a nice attraction to add to the exhibit. He asked if he and his wife could come out and see the horses that evening.

Arriving home I was excited about their visit, but when I walked in the house I noticed that my Westie, MacIntosh was breathing heavy. He had been diagnosed years earlier with a heart condition that was difficult to monitor. Whenever he had a spell I could never get him to the vet in time for them to observe the symptoms. My daughter, Jamie was home. I asked her to keep an eye on Mac while I went to the barn to meet with the Millers.

Lenny and his wife arrived and loved the horses. We sat under the tree outside the barn and he talked about the exhibit. He invited me to bring Magic and Lordi for the entire week of the fair.

They would be in the center of the building housing the exhibit and Lenny himself would take care of them during times I would not be able to be there due to my job. I thanked them for this special opportunity to showcase the Gypsy Vanner Horse. We shook hands and they left. As

I headed down to the house I was high with happiness over this special invitation. Yet, it would be a bittersweet evening.

Upon arriving at the house as I opened the door I found Mac sitting, struggling to breathe, and waiting for me. I scooped him up into my arms and called to Jamie as I grabbed my purse saying I was headed to the vet. Mac rested his head on my arm; his breathing eased now that I held him, but before I even reached my truck he closed his eyes and took his last breath peacefully in my arms. There was no struggle; he had waited to say good-bye. I sobbed deeply; my heart ached. My precious puppy was gone. My vet assured me there was nothing I could have done. It was his heart; he was tired; he loved me as I had loved him; this I knew. I still miss my dog and don't believe I will ever find another to fill this void.

Our Sofie had died while we were in Walden. Her death had been expected over time. She had a parasite found only in the Mediterranean countries. It was not contagious but would eventually take over her organs. It did just that. When it finally took her kidneys we were forced to put her down. She died calmly and peacefully in my arms. As I held my precious Mac; the memory of holding Sofie came back; there was some comfort in the peaceful way they both left this life behind.

Peter loved dogs. He felt my pain and kindly dug a grave for Mac on the corner of the property by the gazebo. It was one of my favorite spots. From the gazebo you could see the Hudson River. It was shady and peaceful there. Peter explained that here other pets were buried. Due to the location no one would ever build on this place; our pets would be safe and undisturbed. There was comfort in that for me.

As I began to prepare Magic and Lordi for their debut at the fair; I still found myself looking down the aisle of the barn expecting to see Mac lying watching me. I began to realize that Mac loved the barn; he loved being there with me as I cared for and groomed the horses. Suddenly my mind realized he was still there; he'd always be there and my memories of him in the barn with me brought a smile.

I went to my Principal, Ed Drozdowski, and told him about the fair. August was a bad time to ask for days off from school. The beginning and ending of a school year are the most harrowing of times; paperwork, schedules, new students and parents, new staff members all need administrative guidance and assistance. However, Ed was supportive of my work with my horses and willingly gave me enough time off to participate in this special project.

My friend, Paula Lynch, had stepped up to help. She was willing to come and cover the booth and keep an eye on my treasures until I could get there. The fair opened and as Lenny had suspected Magic and Lordi were a big hit.

They were so good; loved the attention, and brought to life characteristics that set this breed apart; beauty, intelligence, and an uncanny need to interact with humans.

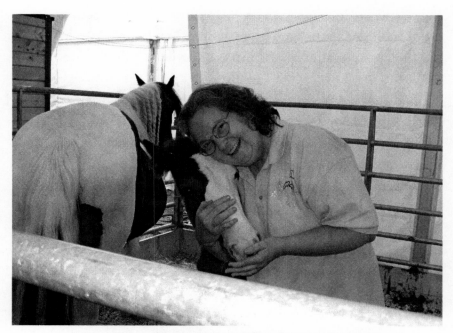

Magic, Me and Lordi at the Dutchess County Fair 2005
(Photo courtesy of Michelle Stalter)

On the last day of the fair is the Draft Horse Show. I had not planned on showing the horses, but Lenny thought it would be great for the spectators to see them in the show ring. He helped me register Magic for the halter class. "What about Lordi?" I asked. "You can bring him in the ring with her", was the reply. I turned to Paula for her experience and help. Paula could do halter classes with her eyes closed. She agreed to show Magic and I would handle Lordi.

A gentle but steady rain had started as we walked the horses to the show ring; we placed fifth in a class of five horses, no matter it was clear who the crowd loved – Lordi! He pranced and trotted along with his mom as if this was something he did regularly. He had a presence; the crowd cheered and applauded; some followed us back to the exhibit area. It didn't matter that Paula and I were wet; we were laughing and smiling; it had been so much fun!

The Dutchess County Fair closed; Jay and Tara came to pick up Magic and Lordi in Tara's trailer. We returned home to the farm on the hill. Bandit and Babes were happy to have Magic and Lordi back. Life was back to normal. If indeed that could ever be said about my life.

Difficulties and change continued to be on life's menu for me in 2006. Even though I casually joked with family and friends about falling down "Alice's rabbit hole", the truth was I felt I had. My life seemed upside down, so much so that it frightened me.

At work I had aimed maybe too high applying for the job of school principal each time my boss either was promoted; forced to move on; or retired. As each left they fully endorsed my desire and attempts to move into the chair they were vacating.

For whatever reason, or reasons, someone else was selected and I found myself facing a new personality; new supervisor, but yet the opportunity to build once again a team to lead the school. Up until coming to West Point my career had been on a solid, positive path; much praise and genuine accolades for jobs well done. I believe this portfolio the reason for being hired for the position at West Point. Yet my hope to bring cutting edge educational techniques to a more traditional educational institution had proved more of a battle ground then I was prepared to face. Now in 2006 not much progress had been made and I found myself not selected for the third and final time and had to begin anew with my new principal.

When this principal arrived on the scene our first meeting was intimidating and confrontational. She sat in a chair and pulled it across the floor into my personal space; we were knee to knee and almost nose to nose as she said, "I know you wanted this job, but I got it." Although over the following three years we worked in the same school and were professionally polite, I know I never recovered from that first meeting.

Her approach to what consisted of a work day and mine were in conflict; her philosophical base was more traditional less willing to brave unproven territory for the sake of improved instruction and so we came to work each day, each week, each month until three years had passed. In my humble opinion no progress for anyone's sake was made.

Maybe it was that rough beginning that over the next three years made me pull away from my life's work and begin to seek a place of service elsewhere. My horses were my sanity through all of this and yet because of what they were I faced another phase of challenge, but one that seemed to whisper opportunity, not just for me but for a community of horse lovers. I am a researcher, an educator to the core. The gypsy culture, this horse, the world of the British equestrians that overlooked it, the Thompsons' work, the establishment of the GVHS, its trials and tribulations were all topics requiring further study and fact gathering for the breed. There existed no textbook, no written resource to check out, review or search for validated information. However, I had found Bandit in a sea of gypsy bred horses; his uniqueness posed questions that drove my curiosity and because of my insatiable need to understand him I had work to do; in spite of the fact that my career of almost thirty years in 2006 was moving towards its close with a degree of unfinished purpose.

My educational energies turned to my horses. I had many times told visitors that you could understand the breed by closely looking at and studying my four Vanners.

Our Magic, our first and the right place to begin. Magic was the larger of my horses; not too large but slightly larger than Bandit. She had sufficient mane, tail and feather and her body was balanced; in proper proportion. Looking closely at her you could without question see the draft horse influence in her heritage. Yet, there was something less drafty there; a refinement was beginning to take form; to change her body components as a new breed was forming through the working of genetic miracles. What genetics? Rudy had not found out her background, so you had to take the gypsy approach to horse breeding in general to evaluate Magic and how she came to be. Over the ten years I had owned this horse I had learned how gypsies had down sized their original draft crosses by introducing the British ponies, particularly the Dales into their breeding programs. I saw few easily recognizable pony characteristics in Magic, but her movement certainly reflected an effortless, somewhat uplifted trot not the heavy more pronounced trot of the draft breeds. She continued to grow up until age five reaching a final height of fifteen hands. When visitors came we always started with Magic then moved on to Bandit.

To this day the reaction is the same when I take this horse out of his stall. Everyone recognizes his distinct beauty. I remember the summer of 06 a lady from my school came out to see the horses, not a horse person or really interested in them, but brought her grandchildren. Her response to Bandit was, "Well, I don't know much about horses but this is one magnificent animal." Over ten years this reaction had been repeated lots I'd even dare to say hundreds of times. I love this horse! He is the breed.

His body, his beautiful head, his hair attributes are just right, not too much, not too little, everything from his head to his tail fits together neatly, naturally complimenting each other. As I talk with interested individuals they see after looking at Magic and then Bandit the elegance that the gypsies moved toward in the breeding process. You can almost see in him how there was less influence of either the draft or pony breeds; that horses possessing these highly desired traits were being bred to each other to maintain and strengthen these; private selectively bred herds of stallions and mares who looked just like Bandit. Ummm.... I thought....wasn't that what the farmer said to Dennis and Cindy Thompson when they stood in the barnyard with him admiring Cushti Bok; "....the gypsy has a band of mares that look just like this little stallion."?

Next the visitor to my barn is introduced to Babes. Ah, my Babes, standing 13.3 hands he reflects the total elegance of the breed as the gypsies continued to down size. Yes, after the mid nineteen nineties when the Thompsons selected the horses to form the GVHS, the gypsy herds had already begun to shift as they continued to breed for the smaller horse. Babes is a product of that shift. He is Bandit only a hand shorter. While some breeders introduced the Dales back into the mix to achieve the smaller size; many of the original families responsible for the Gypsy Vanner breed achieved the shorter horses by simply breeding the smallest breed animal they had to another small breed horse. This last breeding choice produced not only the look but retained the important genetic material that ensured replication time and time again.

And rounding out an educational day at my barn would find you admiring none other than our most loved and spoiled first born, Cushti Bok's Lord Marlborough, lovingly called Lordi. He is a son of Magic and Cushti Bok. He is a replica of his sire only taller. His body is a powerhouse; full and rounded where it needs to be; his movement is "signature" of the breed, smooth, effortless and natural. His head is "sweet" as the gypsies say and his mane, tail and feather are all coming in nicely and in keeping with the growth schedule of fully grown by approximately age five – height and hair complete. He is a first generation Gypsy Vanner Horse. Though he can be mischievous; he is a smart and loving animal like his dam, Magic. He is proof that making the decision to breed Magic on phenotype without known genetics was in this case a good choice. After taking the tour and ending up enjoying Lordi visitors more often than not say that they get it; they see how the breed developed; they see the traits that come from true purebred horses and the reason one would want to reproduce and protect that.

And so I found happiness in the little four stall barn I rented from Peter, sharing my Vanners with those who wanted to see and learn about them. I continued to enjoy working with my horses and preparing them for any exhibit or demonstration that might seek us out. I began to love my weekends which offered more horse time.

"Having been poor is no shame,

but being ashamed of it is."

~ Ben Franklin

On a typical Saturday morning in the fall of '06 I walked Babes as usual up to his paddock. When I released him he ran to the back corner to greet a lady who was walking her dog up through the adjoining apple orchard. As I watched she offered Babes an apple and noticed me.

Reflecting back on this event another fairytale comes to mind…..let's call this happening the beginning of the Snow White effect. Of course at the time I would have had no reason to make such a comparison, yet over the three years that would follow the hand offering the apple would poison friendships, poison people's attitudes towards me, and even make an effort to poison my dream. Out of kindness I invited this woman into my world. What I thought was friendship grew, thus building trust. The form of trust which makes you vulnerable if the person who claims to be a friend……isn't.

I can't begin to understand the changes in my life at the Marlboro farm that developed due to this woman entering the mix of people and personalities there. Change did come and it wasn't in my favor. All my life I had worked hard; paid my way; and done what I believed in my heart was right by others. Yet due to unexplainable circumstances I felt I was losing who I was…who I had always been.

My daughter, her partner, and my less than year old grandson had moved in with me in my tiny one bedroom apartment over the barn.

I had moved from the cottage house to the barn apartment when it became available; another move to try and help reduce my financial stresses. Jill and her family had no place else to go. Peter didn't like this situation. In his defense I have to say though he outwardly disliked it, he tolerated it and allowed them to remain.

I think at this point I had begun to wonder if holding on to my dream with my horses was in the best interest of "what the world would perceive one should do". Most would say if a person has reached the low levels I had, then he/she should see this as a sign and let go of the dream and get back to living life simple though it might be. Every time this kind of thinking occurred I would quickly ask the question, but what about joy....what about life worth living....is that life not what makes one get out of bed in the morning?

I was living in a cramped one bedroom apartment with my daughter and her family; my truck had been repossessed because I failed to make necessary payments (chose rather to have a Christmas); now with no working vehicle, unhappy landlord, the apple lady slowly manipulating opinions and creating discord. Nothing seemed real.

My good friend, Darla, was my shoulder and voice of reason throughout. Darla Monte and her daughter, Dana, had joined my life also because of the horses. Again a woman wanting a horse all her life; sought me out; another Jan Anderson acquired Vanner known as "Armani's Knight in Shining Armor" arrived at only four months old. Darla and Dana loved and spoiled him making him fit right in with my Vanner crew. Darla too found much of my bad luck and unfortunate happenings hard to understand. Never before in my forty plus years had I suffered such hardship and confusion. My escape and place of sanity was in the barn with my horses. They are magical - healing. No matter how deep my pain; how incomprehensible my current moment in time; they took me away from it, made me smile, provided pleasure and somehow I knew they were meant to be in my life. Darla and I would laugh and make "shit" jokes as we mucked stalls. Sometimes we would laugh so hard we would be laughing and crying at the same time. The horses tolerated our craziness; in fact it was as if they encouraged it, knowing that laughter is good medicine. By the time we finished and horses were fed; lights turned out and we were saying our good nights, we both felt things were better and there was a reason to keep believing.

Christmas 2006, just prior to my truck being repossessed, when I was broke and tired was by far one of the best of my life. I certainly believe I enjoyed it the most of all the Christmases spent on the hill. Patti and I had joked about how little money we had yet we both wanted to have Christmas trees. She received a yearly invitation in the mail from a local Christmas tree farm offering a holiday discount. Out of kindness and maybe need Patti invited me to join her in search of Christmas trees for each of us as I had a truck for transporting them home.

Arriving at the tree farm we happily got out and began to look over this year's crop. A chill in the air brought smiles to our faces and a childlike silliness as we asked the man where the smaller, possibly less expensive trees could be found. He pointed to the far field and off we went. The trees were indeed smaller and in some cases quite scraggly.

We began to giggle and make oh poor me jokes which just made us laugh even harder. Suddenly we were looking at two little trees; each with at least "one good side" and a price tag that we liked very much indeed - I believe the trees were $10 each!

We loaded our treasures into the bed of my truck headed home and began to express how perfect this afternoon had been and how much we loved our "Charlie Brown Christmas Trees". I might add that once in our homes they were just right and both filled the small spaces with much joy and holiday spirit.

With that special Christmas behind me; no operating vehicle of my own and undesirable conditions at work I entered 2007. One would think under those circumstances there would be precious little time or sanity to devote to anything else.

Not so, for I have come to recognize I am a woman with a desire to strongly uphold what I believe to be right. Therefore for me, the Gypsy Vanner Horse Society still held a priority. This was important to me. For some this was just a registry; there were now three registries for horses from gypsies; the horses were all the same, right? Well, no. My experience both in Germany and in the USA had taught me clearly that all horses coming from gypsies were not the same; some were definitely "breed" animals and in my opinion should be registered with the GVHS; others were your typical cob horses, indiscriminately bred and more than likely possessed genetics which might not breed true. Others were "Drums" and everyone knew those were crosses between a draft horse and a gypsy horse of some kind. Chat forums were being set up by different groups. Those interested in gypsy bred horses were visiting these groups and joining in the sometimes lively discussion and debate.

The GVHS was under fire. It soon became obvious on the chat forums where I stood and that my stance was unwavering. I hated the twisting of the facts. Dennis Thompson's business dealings of late I had to agree were questionable. Yet, while others took that as reason to erase the GVHS, the name Vanner, and the Thompsons' work to establish the first registry; I would not, simply could not.

I repeatedly defended the importance of their foundational efforts. Those I argued were worth protecting and building on; regardless of Dennis' present path. The name Gypsy Vanner Horse was the pivotal ingredient for the breed. People with no understanding of the Thompsons' work; no understanding of gypsy breeding practices prior to that work; no understanding of the lack of respect for any gypsy bred horse by the British and Irish equestrian communities; those individuals joined right in with the idea that Dennis was a self promoting businessman who made up a name, threw in a few fairytale stories, and was sadly misleading people into buying for huge sums of money what could be had for less – "after all they are all the same horse." These chat rooms were the bowl where the ingredients for disaster for this breed were being mixed daily and at the speed it takes to hit the send button.

At this moment in time I was financially drained, tired and sadly discouraged for my horses. My personal passion had taken sharp blows from people who had far less experience, time, and money invested in these horses. They were becoming the heroines to others whose dealings with Dennis had been hurtful and to the general public's eye appeared vehemently wrong.

While I had to admit portions of their posts were fair accusations, I maintained what Dennis did or was doing at Gypsy Gold was private enterprise and not the Gypsy Vanner Horse Society's business. What he personally chose to do, even though he was the co-founder of the society, should not, nor could it change the foundational events that created the name and the registry. Unless here in America we wanted a hodge-podge of little sturdy cobs indiscriminately bred and only worthy of being recognized as a "type"; we had best remember, write down, embrace and follow the path to the name Gypsy Vanner Horse.

I believe I am both cursed and blessed having found my horses before I knew the Thompsons, Gypsy Gold, or the Gypsy Vanner Horse Society. I had come to understand to a degree the differences among horses bred by gypsies. My search to find and grasp the details of breeding practices that had produced my Bandit led me to the Gypsy Gold website when it first opened. I will never forget the excitement as I read the Thompsons' discovery of Cushti Bok and how they had come over a four year time period to find the breed; to see first hand selective herds that were the birthplace of these horses; to hear from dedicated gypsy breeders their personal journey to breed horses like Cushti Bok and my beloved Bandit not once but consistently over and over again!

I too believed Dennis' business practices of late to be less than in the best interest of everyone. However, within the framework of free enterprise, he had the right to create personal business opportunities as any of us do. In no way did I feel his present business choices should ever negate the amazing steps that had been taken to establish this registry and honor the work of gypsy breeders; those who faithfully shared their knowledge and love of these horses with Dennis and Cindy. This has been and always will be my argument for the sake of the breed when faced with those who wish to make it otherwise. And there were those who wished to make it otherwise. Over time I had come to know many women through these horses. They all were building a following via the chat forums; opinions filled cyberspace clearly reflecting personal agendas.

One individual claiming to be one hundred percent in support of the GVHS and actually was working for the registry at the time called often to talk. Relatively new to the breed as well as the organization she sought to understand some of the history of both. A charming and inquisitive woman I enjoyed sharing what I could to help her with questions she had.

She quickly found supporters among several disenchanted Vanner owners. Sadly, there was a time when all of these women I counted among my friends. Now I was like Alice down the rabbit hole, and was beginning to fear the "f" word – "friend". Given the events at work; the crazy changes in people at the farm; these ladies of cyberspace; and the apple lady.......if these were "friends" then heaven help me should I encounter an enemy!

During the same time period I continued to have frequent conversations with Al Williams who at the time was President of the American Gypsy Horse Breed Association. This organization had been started by Lynn Straumann. Lynn owned Romany's Miss Bodi, one of the original sixteen horses imported by the Thompsons. She lived in California and had done much to promote the Gypsy Vanner Horse out west.

It was Lynn who blazed the trail at many equine venues in her state and area for introducing the Vanner Horse. However, over time more and more folks purchased gypsy bred horses that were not registered with the GVHS. They bought from individuals involved with other registries or from gypsies directly or the larger importers. These folks came with their horses as well to these large events. Lynn being the kind of individual she is was always welcoming and inviting. Everyone got along and enjoyed the horses.

Believing none of the registries were perfect, Lynn toyed with the idea of developing an association, not a breed registry, where everyone and their horses would be welcomed no matter their registry of choice. Everyone could come together all under one umbrella where the horses could be shared and enjoyed. I have to say it was a noble plan.

I understood her thinking; I too was tired of the personal agendas and politics. This was supposed to be about a horse; to understand and protect a rare, new breed that had already been discriminated against in its land of origin. It simply did not need all the confusion and misinformation put out by self promoting individuals. So, brief though it was I joined the AGHBA and volunteered to help.

In fact my friends, Kathy Sommers, Deb Menkens and I, helped Lynn and her sister Robin with the pick-up and transport of the AGHBA's first Angel Baby from quarantine in Newburgh, NY to Ohio. The benevolent work Lynn wanted the AGHBA to accomplish was what had drawn me to the organization. The GVHS, though initially projecting such work, had never been able to get it off the ground. So, I offered to help with the Angel Baby beginnings.

Even so, it did not take long before it became increasingly more difficult for me to do the volunteer work I was attempting to do. Al and Lynn had asked me to help with the educational pieces; brochures on the breed, the organization, etc. The breed brochure was the problem.

Al and I had lengthy telephone conversations on this topic. He did not understand, and he was not alone. Not all gypsy bred horses are a breed; and certainly not "the breed" I had come to know. It was these horses, the breed horses, I wanted desperately for people to grasp and understand. Finally one night I explained to Al I simply could not continue; I could not complete a brochure and not make it sound as if I was explaining and introducing The Gypsy Vanner Horse. The AGHBA was leaning more towards referring to the horses simply as gypsy horses which was more in keeping with their organizational purposes. It was an all inclusive program.

In my opinion, any effort that "grouped any and all horses bred by gypsies" together without understanding the complex reality of the development of those horses that indeed are breed worthy, was not the right way to go at that moment in time. My membership with the AGHBA wasn't renewed. I emailed Al and Lynn to share my decision. I wished them well with the Angel Baby program which I hoped would experience success. With that decision behind me I turned my energies once again to the Gypsy Vanner Horse Society and the work that needed to be done there.

Given my current circumstances just living, inevitably, required most of my day. I had, however, now made a personal promise to my chosen breed and its registry, finding time to give to this work would not be an easy task. Life was becoming more and more complicated.

The apple lady had found a new attention on which to focus – my daughter, Jill. Beautiful, talented, gifted Jill, at age four I discovered her playing the piano by ear. When she took formal lessons I had to remind the teacher to please not play the piece she wanted Jill to practice if she ever wanted my daughter to learn to read music! In Middle School she played the tuba to the delight of our German neighbors. They loved the "um-pa-pa" vibrating through the cul-de-sac each evening. Playing so well as to be asked to move to the High School band two years early; her music instructor also suggested she take lessons from the tuba instructor at the Bremen Symphony.

A fluent German speaker, she found no difficulty in handling two languages. Her closest friends were her German horse friends; with them I believe she found herself; discovered another God given talent; one not tapped before until these beautiful piebald and skewbald horses came floating into an arena and into our lives.

This was the young woman who now was a mother; who continued to struggle within from the pain of the Port Jervis experiences; who had come to me for help. How could such a beautiful and talented young girl as I have described be the same young woman, living with a man incapable of caring for himself let alone his girlfriend and their child? Now he too had found room and board with me. When I stepped back from this scene for a moment all that I knew; all that the world I had lived in my entire life had taught me, said ......trailer trash. God, how in the world had we come to this? The apple lady claiming to want to help had enticed Jill to share personal experiences; the drug days, the death of her boyfriend from an overdose. Jill was vulnerable and trusting. Where she hoped to find advice and support she rather met a woman who twists and mangles truth. Instead of supporting and guiding she accused and belittled.

I was angry with the woman for doing these things. Jill in all the time she had been there with me had helped; she knows these horses; she has a wonderful, natural talent with them. Unfortunately, she doesn't stay motivated long enough to follow through to the level of success she certainly is capable of reaching. Another problem is Jill and I clash. I believe maybe it is because we are much alike; strong willed, determined. For many years we have fought. Only in the last few months have I come to realize the futility in the fussing and fuming. I hope with time and maybe a maturing on both our parts we will move beyond this and be able to share a world with our horses.

Eventually due to the many mishaps and troublesome happenings at the farm, Jill and her family moved in with her partner's family and I found myself in my little apartment with my cats. This was better for the moment. At least there was a quietness that I needed.

Internet forums continued to spew negative chatter regarding the Gypsy Vanner Horse Society. Many felt Mr. Thompson still maintained too much control. It was believed following the 2004 move to officially establish the Gypsy Vanner Horse Society as a non-profit organization; it should be run by a Board of Directors committed to serving the membership. Opinions and suggestions flowed freely. Right smack dab in the middle was the group of ladies, proclaiming Mr. Thompson's evils, and declaring they could possibly be the saviors. They never shared a solution other than the idea of "member driven". I tried to get my mind around the idea. While I could appreciate, and support what I would call "member involvement"; I did not necessarily want our members driving the organization. That is in no way meant to be negative but rather realistic. A young organization with many members who were first time horse owners; many with limited experience in a breed registry; many with a lack of appreciation of the breed, the culture from which it came; and the Thompsons' incredible feat of making this come to pass. How or why would we want those individuals at the helm?

Dennis Thompson founded this organization and introduced these horses to America. It is like giving birth; not many can readily give up the baby and walk away. Certainly not without knowing it is going to be all right; continue to grow in a healthy environment and be well cared for. As I read the ongoing chat room chatter I could understand why he just might be worried things would not fare well for the Gypsy Vanner Horse if *some* members had the chance to be in charge.

This "member driven" idea was catching on as the ladies projected the image of Mr. Thompson as a dictator. After all he was nothing more than an American marketing professional who stumbled across a horse and realized the potential of this rare, beautiful animal. He slapped a name on it; took it from the gypsies and there you have it. Surely, he is the bad guy, and the women of cyberspace will take him on and save not only the horse but the gypsies as well!

I felt I had to go online and follow the dialogue if I was to remain true to my promise, but with time this became a dreaded chore. I was still receiving phone calls from several women, acquaintances because of the horses. All wanting to know what I thought about everything being discussed in chat rooms and what could be done? I wanted them to back off; I wanted Dennis to play fair; and I wanted everyone to recognize the truth with regards to this breed. While there may be some questionable things in anyone's story, I believe the truth as best it could be found in the early 1990's with regards to this horse was uncovered by Dennis and Cindy Thompson. By establishing the GVHS with sixteen identified selectively bred horses as the foundation, they not only recognized but saved the breed. The gypsies did not stop doing what they have always done; making changes and seeing what else they can accomplish through breeding both indiscriminately and selectively. The selective herds of 2010 are very different from those first encountered by the Thompsons; the horses are much smaller; the heads reflect a strong pony influence in some herds probably because of a reintroduction of the Dales into the breeding process. While some gypsy breeders have successfully created a twelve hand Vanner! That achieved by breeding smaller Vanner to smaller Vanner and finally having a pony sized Vanner – all the traits, all the wonderful looks, but standing only twelve hands!

Yet, in late 2007 there was no one listening to this information; they simply wanted to bring down Dennis Thompson. By so doing they would also do away with or most certainly cast doubt on the name, Gypsy Vanner Horse. In which case the slate would be clean and they would then be in a position to call this horse whatever "they" wanted to. They could dub themselves founders.

There were nights after spending an hour either reading the terrible emails, or getting off the phone from talking with one of these women that I would either shut off the computer, or hang up the phone and run downstairs to the barn and stare into the stalls. Again, my horses would validate for me that they were not just any horse bred by gypsies; they were not like the ordinary cobs often seen on the roads and byways as one travels through England; no, as the gypsy who sold me Bandit had said, ...he is a one of a kind; there are not that many if any like him......if he has your heart he does not belong to me any longer." Why would a gypsy who had bred such a horse say this if there were herds of horses just like this one roaming around right outside Heathrow (as one email once stated). No, I knew better. I'd been through Heathrow, not once but many times. I was angry. It seemed to me all of these individuals wished they had been the one who found the horse and built the breed registry. They were angry with Dennis Thompson, because secretly they all wished they had done what he had done.

I was also angry with Dennis. Much too often he set himself up for their attacks. While some saw his "Certification Program" (a private program offering from Mr. Thompson his personal guarantee that the horse they owned was indeed a Gypsy Vanner Horse) as just another money-making scheme, in reality it was his attempt to once again save the breed. In 2003 when he opened the registry to allow horses meeting the breed standard by phenotype only this was both good and bad. Good because there were horses that should have been included and as long as Mr. Thompson kept the registry private it was difficult to register such horses. On the other hand there were horses making it into the registry once the door was opened that should not have.

The hope for one registry for the breed was still there; the 2003 meeting in Ohio had tried, failed; now in 2007 the idea was being resurrected. Why? If there was one registry; one breed; then all gypsy bred horses could be grouped together just like they are in their homeland? Isn't that the way the gypsies do it?

No, actually they know the differences and do separate the horses. It takes time and the building of an almost "like family" relationship with them before you get them to explain not only how they separate but why. The Thompsons certainly knew this but not without four years of constant interaction, searching, and building the necessary level of trust with those families. Due to that work, now gypsies, not just gypsies with selective herds, but I fear any gypsy with a horse was coming forward to get in on the action. Now that is the gypsy way!

With the internet and the allure of these horses from this "mysterious and enchanting" culture the doorway for large scale buying and selling had been thrown wide open. Gypsies were now available and befriended the chat room ladies who now with "gypsy friends" claimed a degree of expertise with regards to the breed.

The GVHS was holding an election; three Board of Director seats were open.

I had decided if I was going to take a stand on behalf of my beloved breed – the Gypsy Vanner Horse then I needed to do it now! I announced I was running in the election and I carefully completed the required questionnaire. Then one night a call came from the charming and inquisitive lady. She asked me not to run. Seems the ladies had determined that should I run I would take votes away from their chosen candidates. Naturally they wanted their candidates to win those seats; making a majority on the Board and enabling changes that had been openly discussed on the chat forums to take place. I was in the way; and when I refused to comply with their wishes they began a heavy duty phone campaign to elect their friends. It worked for them. Their candidates won and would take office on 1 January, 2008.

In December 2007 the GVHS Board of Directors took actions that have been viewed by some as unscrupulous. A respected Director was removed for what was considered a conflict of interest. It was a conflict of interest I had come face to face with, recognized and resolved in favor of supporting the GVHS. It was with heartfelt frustration I hated to see her go, but because I had been there, because I too saw this conflict my frustration changed to disappointment. A newly elected Director was removed for written attacks against the GVHS via the internet. Another resigned. All of these swift changes took place from 1 January through early February. I had been asked to accept a Board seat since I had received the next highest number of votes in the recent election.

The chat attacks began – vicious, mean, and hateful. I was already an enemy because I stood up for the Thompsons' work and the name Gypsy Vanner Horse; now I was further hated because I had been willing to take a leadership position under what some called questionable circumstances.

Oh and like in the children's nursery rhyme the dish ran away with the spoon; the GVHS Registrar ran away with the records; holding them hostage; all a part of what could have been a takeover and ultimate downfall of this registry. While I believe most of these ladies would deny or say that is not how it happened; these are the events and suggest an underhanded approach that could have come to no good, be it a planned takeover or just a shift in power leading to changes in favor of "members" rather than "the breed."

The GVHS was on shaky ground. Hateful and accusatory emails continued to fly about from one chat forum to another. It was crazy. There was a lot of work to do to get back on track; to turn the focus back to the horse. The GVHS is a "breed" registry not a "member" registry. Please understand I in no way am down playing members and their importance in any organization; but members join an organization for a purpose – not just to be a member. The purpose of the GVHS is the breed – its recognition, protection, and promotion. If this is not your purpose then why would you want to be a member of this organization? If you are a member would you not want this to be what your leadership spends its time and energy doing?

It was nearing the time for the GVHS Annual Meeting (February 2008). I asked if I could form a Steering Committee to assist with the preparations for the meeting. Anne Crowley, Robin Visceglia, and Rhonda Cofer came to my aid. They worked so hard; prepared all the meeting folders and materials; and most importantly provided the encouragement I needed to even get on the plane to go to Texas.

The trip to Texas had started with a snow storm drive from my friend Kathy Sommers' house to Newark International. Actually it was a blinding blizzard; the snow was coming down so fast and hard I could barely see the road. Seeing no other cars or even trucks lead me to realize we were probably the only fools out in this. However, determined to get to Texas we pressed on. Kathy had decided to accompany me claiming it to be an opportunity to visit her sister. Deep down I knew she was coming along to keep me safe; to befriend me if things went awry. We made it to the Newark airport and checked in only to sit on the tarmac for a very lengthy delay. As we waited in the plane we thought maybe we should heed these signs; just get off the plane and return to the warmth and safety of home. We were de-iced twice! I secretly thought as the green gook flowed over the window that is what this trip was all about; we were headed to help de-ice the GVHS and get it back on track. Finally we were allowed to take off – the plane pushed through the heavy clouds exiting into the bright sunshine above.

Once at the hotel I was greeted by the Steering Committee (Anne, Robin, Rhonda) and Kim Osborne who was there to help too. Their energy and dedication renewed my frozen spirit and we buckled down and got to work stuffing folders and sharing stories that made us smile and enjoy the important work we were doing.

This was not going to be an easy meeting. Dissatisfied members had created quite a ruckus; looking at Dennis as being the GVHS; carrying a ton of blame and threatening to sling it to get what they wanted. A question and answer session had been scheduled prior to the meeting to give any and all the opportunity to hear answers from the GVHS Board of Directors – Dennis Thompson, Bill Ricci and me. The Golden Geldings seemed to be a point of contention.

When the Thompsons formed the GVHS, Cindy Thompson had much wanted to establish a means of sharing the Vanners through benevolent work and donating geldings to therapeutic centers, equine assisted educational work, etc. The skeleton for that program was written; Cindy's untimely death prevented it from becoming a reality. Yet, within that framework a percentage, of membership fees, was to go to that program and it still remained as a line item on the budget. Geez, paperwork, especially for this registry had been a nightmare; the ones responsible for the record keeping had changed multiple times since the beginning. The transitions were not always smooth ones. However, the faces wanting answers and looking to Dennis, Bill and me were not kind and in no way did they think they should be forgiving.

The GVHS Treasurer had explained no money was going into that program nor was Mr. Thompson receiving anything from the program as it no longer existed. With that explained they went on to other concerns and we answered as best we could under the present organizational structure and status. The session ended and everyone was reminded of the start time for the Annual Meeting.

The Annual Meeting got underway with no difficulty. The unhappy campers from the previous session did not return. That said a lot. If you really have a concern with the organization you attend the Annual Meeting to ensure the total membership becomes aware. Yet, they did not come; for me that said their agenda was personal not organizational.

The GVHS members who attended the Annual Meeting came with a genuine concern for the health and well being of their chosen registry. They had read the chat room threats and listened to the forceful unwarranted demands. They worried that those would be the ones to move on with the breed and this they did not want. They came to stand up for the Gypsy Vanner Horse and the only registry formed to recognize and protect it – it was their investment, their future, they came to ask what they could do.

GVHS President Bill Ricci called the meeting to order. Items on the agenda were discussed and addressed. Dennis Thompson spoke passionately about this registry. He did not speak as someone wanting personal recognition rather he spoke about the original intent – the recognition and promotion of a breed. He shared his personal regret for the troubles we as an organization faced. I had asked to be given the opportunity to share my personal understanding of the breed and my support of the GVHS. I prepared a short PowerPoint highlighting and reminding those present that not all horses bred by gypsies are a breed; this complex truth has to be understood, embraced and honored.

As I closed my presentation I thanked everyone for coming, and challenged them to accept the responsibility of respecting and promoting the mission and goals of the GVHS. The smiles, the applause, and even a few stray tears were my affirmation.

When that group of GVHS members left Texas, they left with a renewed dedication and faith in the Gypsy Vanner Horse Society. They also knew we would all have to work together to reclaim what could quickly be lost with regards to the breed.

With a sense of hope and a renewed determination to work harder to help educate about the Vanner breed, Kathy and I flew back to NY and the uncertainties still surrounding my life at the farm on the hill and at school.

**Jill on Bandit at the Goshen NY Historic Harness Racing Track.
We participated in a Parade of Breeds that day.**

The GVHS was now headed in a more positive direction; I was filled with a sense of purpose with the work I wanted to do there. Also, there was a shift for the better in my personal life - could it be things were starting to look up? I was slowly chipping away at my mountain of debt. Hope was returning, and I believed many aspects of my life were improving. During '07 I had been without a vehicle. I had borrowed one from a fellow teacher and then from none other than the apple lady which as you can guess was a mistake.

In January 08 another divine intervention, a Jeremiah 29:11 experience, occurred and this is how it happened.....I was as I said slowly getting bills paid off, yet my credit score remained inadequate to purchase a vehicle (probably even a bicycle; don't know didn't try). I began to share with friends my desire for a good, used car/truck; just as long as it would run and get me to and from work. It also needed to be in a price range where I could pay cash given my credit rating.

Brian Krutchkoff, a horse friend called. A Ford dealership he worked closely with through his business had a clunker truck for $500. The mechanic had assured Brian though the body needed work the engine was in excellent shape. The truck would be safe and sounded as if it would serve my needs at present.

The next day I arrived at the dealership and was warmly greeted by the salesman. This was certainly a change for me. My troubles of late had me programmed for disappointment and unkind treatment, yet here was a smile, a handshake, and a friendly welcome.

He invited me to come along as we walked out to his waiting car. We would have to drive over to their used car lot to see the truck. I remained anxious, I expected his mood to change any minute, I was being treated as if I was buying one of their top of the line models; not a $500 clunker. We reached the lot; he continued his friendly salesman talk as we drove up and down the lines of parked cars. Finally he took his cell phone and spoke to a colleague. I listened as he explained we were unable to find the truck… a series of "uh-huh's" followed and he hung up. The truck had been sold that morning by his unknowing colleague. He offered a sincere apology.

"Not a problem", I said. However, inside I was thinking this is more like it; how things work for me. We drove up the last line of cars in the lot towards the exit. He stopped just short of the exit in front of a nice Ford F-150; navy blue, chrome trimmings – nice truck. He asked what I thought of this one. I replied, "I like it, but am certain I cannot afford it just yet."

"Let's look at it anyway", he encouraged getting out of the car. I joined him. Opening the door he invited me to try it out. I stepped up into the cab – it was perfect. My hands rested on the steering wheel as he rambled on about it being a 1999 special edition model. I let him talk; I daydreamed for a moment.

Then realistically I replied, "I love it, but as I said I cannot afford, nor will my current credit score support the necessary loan, but thank you. I really appreciate what you are trying to do."

Returning to the dealership I expressed again my thanks suggesting that if another "excellent clunker" came in to please let me know. The salesman did not want to give up and asked if I would just have a seat at his desk for a moment he wanted to check out any and all possibilities for me to get the F-150.

Okay, I could sit once more in front of the desk while he searched on the computer, talked on the phone…..then wait for the only possible reply, "Yes, unfortunately you are correct. It just can't be done now." Suddenly, his voice interrupted my thoughts as I heard him say, "I'll be right back. I have to check with my manager."

I watched as the two men talked briefly, looking back at me once, while I tried reading their lips, their minds…..(sure, Charlie, the lady with that score wants a loan – don't think so).

I had reached that place where you don't believe anymore. While down the rabbit hole I had lost hope. I looked down at my lap and sighed. During the now painful wait I uttered a short prayer, "Dear God, do You think I could have the truck?"

Again brought back to reality by the salesman's kind voice I looked up, smiled and said, "I'm sorry what did you say?"

"I said, you can have the truck, my manager called in a favor. We want to help you", he said with an understanding smile.

All American Ford in Hackensack, NJ had just become the first rung on the ladder out of the hole. I signed all the paperwork thinking all the while of my friend, Brian and knowing he was behind this; he had made this possible for me. I explained I would be back to pick up the truck as soon as my daughter could bring me.....MY TRUCK!! WHEE-HA!! On the drive back home I laughed, I cried, and I thanked God for this new beginning. I was Joyce, not Alice anymore!

Bandit and me with Judy at The Dutchess County Fair, Rhinebeck, NY.

My friendship with Carliss Henderson had continued to grow. Since '06 we had been discussing the possibility of a farm partnership once

I retired. She and her husband, Jerry, had invited me to visit them and I had agreed combining our herds and building a breeding business would be fun and support what I hoped to achieve for the breed. We originally had planned to expand at the farm the Henderson's first purchased, but as my retirement grew closer, and surrounding property owners chose not to sell, it became apparent we really needed to look for a new location. Carliss began checking out the possibilities and I looked forward to her nightly calls to discuss our future.

Spring of '08 continued to be one of highs and lows; but the highs were more numerous and promising. It was the first season of foals by my stallion, Babes. He had bred my friend Dianna Guldjberg's mare, Shaylee. The foal was a beautiful filly! Dianna, friend Linda Sibilia, and their trainer were all present for the late afternoon birth.

I had known Dianna and Linda for a long time. We met at a driving competition in New Jersey. My driving trainer, Susan Skipper, was showing Equirace Gypsy (ER), a Gypsy King daughter owned by Amy Peltz. It was a rainy day and I had decided not to bring Bandit and was helping Susan.

Sitting on the front row of bleachers while Susan and ER were in the ring I was joined by two ladies, Dianna and Linda. They introduced themselves and began talking about ER, a Gypsy Vanner they were seeing in person for the first time – excitement was evident. My friendship with Dianna and Linda grew over the years. They even showed up wearing T-shirts and proclaiming to be "Joyce Groupies" in March 2007 at Lord Sterling Stables where with Darla, Dana and Jill we did a Gypsy Vanner Horse demonstration and seminar with Bandit and Magic before a standing room only crowd. For Shaylee to have Babes' first foal was indeed a celebration for all of us! Dianna shared during Shaylee's labor a single bird was heard singing a uniquely beautiful melody. Later when she asked what I thought would make a good name we talked about the song and words she had found in the Romany language. Together we chose the name, "Shaylee's Bevin" which means, "The Fairy Princess' Lady With Song".

Babes' second foal would be born to my Magic; another beautiful filly. This one had been purchased inutero by the apple lady; paid for by a loan, use of her car; and with reluctance a small additional amount after the birth. The arrival of this foal certainly brought joy, another beautiful Babes' daughter. However, the difficulties that followed could not have been foreseen. The foal, at only a few days old, slipped and fell while in the paddock with Magic. She chipped a stifle bone. The series of events that followed were a nightmare. As any responsible breeder would do I offered to buy back the foal following the injury, but the woman refused. Instead she built an entire website painting me to be a villain. While I could fill pages with my version of the story, I see no need. I invited her into my world with my horses as I invite people in today. My only purpose was then and is as always to share the truly wonderful Vanner Horse; to let it work its magic on those who have come to interact with it. To finish out Babes' first foal crop a third filly was born to Lise McNamara's mare, Fiona. Three fillies, I was very pleased with this stallion and his lovely daughters.

Towards the end of the summer '08 I received a call from Dianna, I could hear the distress in her voice. A family crisis was brewing she would be forced to sell her horses and she was worried about Bevin. She wanted her to go to a home that would respect who she is. Without a doubt I thought I'd love to have Bevin; but how could I? Financially I was just beginning to come out of my debt. Then I remembered Kathy had mentioned the possibility of owning a Vanner as an investment. I called her. Kathy too had encountered similar family difficulties and suddenly it was not just about an investment but also about helping a woman who needed other women to support and give her courage. Kathy's friend, Allyson Pritchard, had begun to find interest in my Vanner passion. Kathy called Allyson and asked if she too would like to help. Before we knew it Kathy and I were driving to Jersey to visit Dianna. For Kathy, seeing Bevin was love at first sight; Allyson trusted our decision. Kathy and Allyson gifted Bevin to me for safe keeping, training, future showing and breeding. It has become a real "First Wives Club" adventure; one we hope will last a very long time filled with much celebration for each of us as well as the breed. Bevin was photographed by equine photographer, Mark J. Barrett and appears with friend, Dorothy Cleary's filly, Twink, in Mark's 2011 Gypsy Vanner Horse Calendar.

Another truly magical experience occurred towards the end of summer '08. I received a call from Vanessa Wright, a photographer who wanted to take pictures of my horses for a special project she was conducting. As Vanessa explained the project I could not help but get excited. Not only was Vanessa a photographer but she was a teacher. Her project, "The Literary Horse", used lovely photos of horses with their humans to make connections to treasured works of literature. Using public libraries as the exhibit halls for this wonderful project brought people back to the world of books and the amazing stories that should never be forgotten or lost. Vanessa came and spent an entire day with us and the horses; it was a day that I will remember always; it was filled with enchantment and the photos Vanessa took that day reveal the magic. Not long after the photo shoot Vanessa emailed me. I still get a little teary eyed recalling that message. It stated that out of all the over 20,000 photos she had taken for the project a photo she had taken of me with my beloved Bandit had captured the essence of the project like no other. She had decided to use this particular picture as the official invitation photo for The Literary Horse. It is me sitting next to Bandit reading to him while he is lying down in his stall. The caption reads, "Once upon a time is happening right now....." I was indeed honored to have her choose this photo. The one thing I know for certain is, that my Vanners have and continue to bring "once upon a time" moments into my life - there is no way to be around them and not sense the magic.

Also in summer 2008, a young trainer had taken the apartment behind Patti's. She had helped with my young stallion, Lordi, and joined in for lots of fun with Darla, Dana, Jill and our horses. After showing our horses at the Dutchess County Fair we learned that she had a student interested in boarding her horse at the farm. Tara, my landlord's daughter, had stopped by to say she did not feel this would be good. The farm was about at its limit for horses and so she would prefer that the new boarder not come. The trainer seemed fine with that decision. Until a few days later.......

Darla and I were enjoying an unseasonably warm evening as we walked down from the upper barn after finishing up with Armani. We were laughing and I was thinking how nice it was to finish early. I was looking forward to making a light meal and enjoying an old movie.

Suddenly we saw Jay, coming up through the paddock with a young girl. I recognized her; it was Rachel, the trainer's student. We all said hello. Jay shared that he had just picked up Rachel's horse and she would be boarding in the stall next to Armani in the upper barn. Darla and I were both puzzled. Darla, who wants everything on the up and up, asked if Rachel had the horse's current Coggins and shot records. She said no, but she could get them. Jay on the other hand went into defense mode – angry, yelling. Darla and I asked if we could all meet over by Peter's pool and talk this out. Everyone went in opposite directions; Darla and I went to the pool. Rachel went to get the trainer who came in her pajamas; indicating she didn't know anything about this. Jay had gone directly to Peter then joined us announcing Peter had no objections.

I went to see Peter, who was sitting on a counter stool staring at his computer; he seemed agitated that I couldn't just let the girl have her horse here. I tried to diplomatically explain the problems this would cause primarily because we were not prepared to take the horse this evening. The stall the horse was to use was at present a run-in for my stallion, Babes.

Outside time would be a problem as Armani and Babes used the paddock adjoining the little barn; each turned out separately due to Babes

135

being a stallion. We would need to rethink turnout. I also was concerned with Rachel's inability to provide proper health documents.

Long story – short – Darla and I helped clean out the run-in; got shavings; asked at least if the horse had been wormed and what schedule it was on. Again, not able to provide this information; we provided a wormer and administered it to the horse for her. And this was just the beginning.......enough has been shared that I will simply say I began to look at moving my horses to the Henderson's farm in Louisiana as soon as was possible.

In the Fall of '08 Magic, Bandit, and Lordi were sent to Belle Rose Farm in Monroe, Louisiana until I could retire and join them there. Babes and Bevin remained with me. Darla moved Armani down to join them in the little four stall barn I called home. Life went on around us; we enjoyed our Vanners together. We laughed, joked, and looked for peace in that little barn.

My work at school was nothing more than passing time; there was no reward. I went to work each day; did what was required; and was grateful when it was time to leave. I hated to see what was happening under the current leadership. I saw dissatisfied staff, teachers, parents and students – it was very disturbing to me. Even though I had sought the help and intervention of superiors, nothing was done. Retirement began to be eagerly anticipated and longed for.

While my career was coming up short and leaving me feeling empty, my work with the GVHS brought purpose and focus back to my life. I was so very thankful for the Board of Directors that formed following the 2008 Annual Meeting. The combination of dedication, expertise, and resources had revitalized the organization. Our attention had returned to the standard of excellence on which this registry was founded. Taking a careful look at the breed standard we realized this is where we needed to concentrate our work.

Director Michael Litz contacted equine professional, Wayne G. Hipsley. Mr. Hipsley was a respected judge and had served many breed organizations in a variety of positions. He had written breed standards for several of those organizations and we now sought his expert advice and assistance. As 2008 was drawing to a close, a clarified breed standard had been achieved. Mind you, not changed; in no way did we want our original standard changed, just put into a language equine professionals could better understand when trying to grasp the expected quality the GVHS demands in the Vanner Horse.

Suddenly I found myself using my skills as an educator within the framework of my passion for this breed. I had volunteered to write the affiliate news article for the Equine Journal each month; this I had been doing for some time. I also had published an article in American Livestock Magazine. As these things were accomplished I began to realize my dream again; I had almost lost it as well as the desire to fulfill it while down the rabbit hole.

While enduring those hardships brought on primarily by debt and financial struggles money became a focal point. Money was the only thing of value. Maybe this is why the Bible says, "Money is the root of all evil." In reality it holds the least value when achieving real joy and satisfaction. When at my lowest; feeling if I just had money I could eliminate my problems; I was faced with whether to sell my horses. I couldn't go there; I chose rather to do without many comforts to hold on to what had the greatest of value – my future with my horses. With time things improved and the reality of just how powerful holding on to a dream is became crystal clear; it also grew hope and gave me the ability to take a long close look at what else I could do with the gift I had been given.

As healing was returning to my life I became aware of unusual events; one might even consider there was a little magic involved; all adding to my growing sense of happiness and well being. On a typical school day in the late fall of 2007 one of the teachers had assigned her students a research project on myths and legends. Knowing I loved unicorns she sent the "unicorn group" to me. Rather than answer their questions I asked them to follow me to the library where we could do a little research. Books on unicorns were placed on a table for us and we began to search through them. One book caught my attention; its illustrations were captivating and almost invited you into them; they seemed so real. The book was, <u>*Where Have All the Unicorns Gone*</u> by Jane Yolen and illustrated by Ruth Sanderson. After the students returned to their class I checked out the book and took it to my office. I turned to the back flap where a brief bio was written on the author and illustrator. To my surprise Ruth Sanderson lived close by in Massachusetts. An email address was provided and I sent her a message. I simply thanked her for the beautiful paintings that captured a personal interest – the unicorn. I shared I owned a rare horse, the Gypsy Vanner and always saw them as having traits often associated with unicorns. In her illustrations I saw both Vanner and unicorn – just lovely. Never did I expect a reply.

However, there it was when I opened my email the next day – a message from Ruth Sanderson. She thanked me for my email and shared she too loved horses. In fact she was beginning work on a new series and had wished she knew someone involved with Gypsy Vanners. The breed she thought might be a nice addition to the ones already chosen for the series. She said she was filing my email address for future reference. I was honored and excited. About a month later I received an invitation to the grand opening of her art studio in Palmer, Massachusetts. It would be right before Christmas and she would have many of her items on sale at the event. I ran quickly to share this with Kathy Sommers, my friend and librarian, and asked if she would like to go with me.

On that December day two excited book lovers were on their way to see a favorite children's book illustrator; also a fellow horsewoman. We found the studio; smells of spices and refreshments added holiday cheer while visitors wandered around the gallery in admiration of the work on display. Kathy and I purchased books for Christmas gifts and waited until Ruth was free to say hello and have her sign the books. She greeted me as the "Gypsy Vanner Lady"; was obviously pleased I had come. We were introduced to her husband and daughter and invited to stay for a special concert with guitarist, Francis Doughtery – a birthday gift from her husband. We accepted and had a delightful afternoon. As we were saying our good-byes she said she would love to use Vanners in a work sooner than waiting to include them in the series, which was uncertain. She then asked if I knew of anyone having a Vanner baby in the spring. Kathy and I looked at each other – "My mare is", I replied. She then told us of Jane Yolen's latest project, a lullaby book. Ruth was doing the illustrations and they were of mares and foals. She asked if she could use my mare as a model for one of the two page layouts for this book. Joyful tears could not be contained – Magic in a Ruth Sanderson painting - dreams do come true!

I love books and began to spend time reading again; something that had fallen by the way side as I became overwhelmed by difficulties. Now, I found encouragement once again from authors who had faced similar struggles or simply wanted to share their counsel with interested readers. While visiting the local Barnes and Noble bookstore a display grabbed my attention. The book was, _The Dream Manager_, by Matthew Kelly. I picked it up; read the intro and hurried to the counter to buy it. Over the next couple of days I devoured the work. School, my career of twenty-nine years, was an empty place now. Not just for me but for several of my colleagues and I wanted to find ways to bring them out of this slump. Mr. Kelly suggested that in a business environment employees are much more productive if they see their work as a means to an end. When that end is a "personal dream" the production is significantly greater. His work is about managing in such a way as to make that possible; assisting employees in identifying and then actively pursuing those dreams – the company and the employee both win.

I could completely understand this philosophy. I had begun to see just how energized I was becoming as I followed after my dream of owning and breeding Gypsy Vanner Horses while using them in therapy and equine assisted education programs – a marriage of career and passion. If people were not only given the opportunity, but encouraged in their work place to pursue their dreams openly and vigorously, what amazing good would result. I emailed Mr. Kelly and thanked him for the encouragement I received from his work. I received a response which I copied and placed on a bulletin board in my office. The title on the board was "Believe in your dreams"; a favorite poster of a unicorn rearing underneath a rainbow adorned the board. In the center was my Ruth Sanderson unicorn calendar; to the side a copy of my first email from Mrs. Sanderson and now it was joined by Mr. Kelly's message.

This board made me smile each morning as I entered my office and reminded me of my future, my hope and God's promise to me, "For I know the plans I have for you declares the Lord, plans to prosper you and not to harm you, plans to give you hope and a future. – Jeremiah 29:11. I truly believed for the first time in a long time that I was beginning to have hope and was heading toward that promised future.

In February 2009 I flew to Lexington, Kentucky for the Annual Meeting of the Gypsy Vanner Horse Society. Excitement filled the air as this would be the first GVHS Breed Seminar conducted by Wayne G. Hipsley for judges as well as breeders and enthusiasts. Barb Snyder had done an incredible job making all the arrangements; Mike and Pam Litz had put together all the seminar binders and had everything ready. We had a good turn out. The Board was pleased and began to make arrangements for the next seminar which hopefully would include a horse evaluation. I was so happy to be a part of this journey; to see the progress that was being made to not only understand and recognize this breed, but to genuinely preserve and promote it as it should be.

2009 was turning out to be a travel year for me. Shortly after returning to New York following the GVHS meeting I was headed south to Louisiana to visit Carliss. It was March and spring was well underway when I arrived in Monroe. I loved the south and the warm weather that brought relief to my arthritis pain. It was so good to see

Bandit, Magic and Lordi. I truly had missed them, but Carliss had taken such good care they were all fat and happy. The big goal this trip was to help Carliss look at and choose a possible relocation site for Belle Rose Farm. A local realtor, Parker Wilkes, had a few places for us to see. One was a beautiful piece of property on rolling hills in the West Monroe area. Unfortunately we could only afford fifteen acres and the way the land was situated it would have been difficult to place our barn, arena and house given the number and slope of the hills. So off we went to the next place, this was an area Carliss had found through another realtor. It was in Sterlington in Morehouse Parish. We had to drive over a quaint little bridge with a sign that read, "Welcome to the Island – Bartholomew Subdivision".

The road wound through a well manicured residential area at the end was a dirt road to the right. Here the trees on either side stretched their limbs towards each other making almost a canopy of green under which we drove. We had to take the second left, another dirt road and finally found ourselves looking out over twenty-three acres of flat, lovely land – right in the middle of an island surrounded by Bayou Bartholomew. It seemed a perfect farm site for two little old ladies who did not want to have to go up and down hills to turn out or bring in horses from paddocks. We would over time look at a couple more places, but we always came back to the island. When I left to return to NY Carliss and I had reached the decision the island would be the best location for the farm.

Arriving back in NY my thoughts now had to turn to finishing out the school year and making the move to Louisiana at the end of July, early August. I had talked with Kathy about possibly moving in with her for the last couple of months and getting away from the farm which simply was no longer a good or comfortable place for me and my animals. Fortunately, Deb Menkens, a teacher and horse friend, had a lovely barn not far from Kathy's. Deb was kind enough to offer a place for Babes and Bevin to stay until I was ready to take them down to Louisiana. Things were coming together because of friends and I was most grateful.

Carliss and I had decided we needed to buy a horse trailer rather than have Babes and Bevin shipped to Louisiana. It just made sense; eventually we would have to have one with all the horses we owned; might as well be now. Again, fate was kind. Darla called to tell me Paul Congelosi had a wonderful used EXISS three horse trailer for a reasonable price. I called and went out after work to see it. It was like new had everything I had ever wanted except a ramp. When I explained I'd like it if it had a ramp, the salesman said that was easy enough. They could just add one if they had one in stock. He called back to have someone check storage. When the return call came it was to tell us they only had one ramp in stock and it was the one for this trailer. I just smiled. I took this as a sign, called Carliss and made arrangements to drop off my truck to have the fifth wheel installed the next day.

Now with my own trailer, I made arrangements and took Babes and Bevin over to Deb's the beginning of May. I informed Peter that I was moving out. I did away with most of my furniture as the plan was to share the house with Carliss and Jerry. I just packed up my knick knacks, books, pictures, and treasures from all my travels and stored them at a local storage company for the time being. Off I went with my three cats, Jack, Artemus and Paws, to Kathy's leaving the farm on the hill behind me; I don't believe I looked back as I left Marlboro. Where it had been a place of great happiness in the beginning it had become a place of sadness; of hurtful situations forced on me without reason. I would remember the good times through Lordi; he would always have Peter and Tara's name; a name given to him to honor the original kindness shown me when I first arrived. It was those times I would try and remember.

My last three months in New York I was not well. I had a terrible flare of my arthritis and sometimes just getting out of bed in the morning was extremely painful; maybe just from the stress of all the changes. Yet, somehow I managed going over to Deb's each morning to care for Babes and Bevin before heading off to work. At school there was much talk of end of year parties, closing school and celebrating the upcoming retirements. I had such delightful friends at West Point; truly fine people, excellent educators, wonderful parents and students who indeed were a pleasure to serve. I count among my blessings the opportunity to have been able to be a part of the West Point community for the last eight years of my career. To be able to serve at this prestigious and historical school was indeed a highlight of my thirty years with the Department of Defense.

Though the Middle and Elementary school staffs hosted a formal retirement party and the Superintendent's office held one in Virginia for us as well; my favorite party was given at the home of Audrey Butler, a teacher extraordinaire, and one of the most genuine human beings I have ever met. The party was for me; the people who came were my friends; they had worked with me as an educator, as an administrator, yet that wasn't why they were there. They came to this party to say they cared; they wanted to wish me well; they all understood my personal dreams and they wanted to cheer me on. As my eyes scanned their faces I wanted to remember them all, these were the people I would miss. It would be these friends I would think about when my time in NY came to mind. I would hope the very best for them and wish successes in their future endeavors in the same way they had come to bid me a fond farewell. When it came time for sharing gifts we enjoyed each little remembrance, but the one that made me really smile was from Audrey. Trying to get home for the party she had stopped at McDonalds for a quick lunch with her grown son, who asked for a "Kids Meal". She obliged, but asked him if she could have the enclosed toy when she saw what it was. She handed me a little gift bag. I peeled back the tissue paper and nestled therein was a tiny white unicorn with purple mane, tail, and feet. A little manufacturer's tag was attached and I opened to find the following: "FABLE" was the name and then there was this verse:

"Let your imagination explore
An amazing land of mystical lore,
As long as you can wish and believe
All of your dreams you are bound to achieve."

I made a promise to my friends gathered there; if my dream ever landed me a spot on Oprah, they would all be invited to be in the audience. Leaving the party I thanked them all again, and said I'd see them in Chicago which brought smiles and laughter.

Before I knew it June had arrived. It was time to trailer Babes and Bevin down to Louisiana. Kathy had graciously agreed to come along and be the second driver. I wanted to drive straight through making the trip as easy as possible on the horses.

We picked them up at Deb's farm. I thanked her for her kindness once again and we were off. I was a bit anxious having never trailered horses further than NY to PA; now we were headed all the way down south! We stopped every three hours and offered the horses hay and water; they were so good. They drank their water, welcomed our pats and loves, and hungrily accepted filled hay nets. Kathy and I switched back and forth; we chatted, tried to think of funny things, freed each other for nap breaks, but kept right on truckin' as they say. I was so happy when we crossed into Mississippi. We pulled into the "Welcome to Mississippi Rest Area". I have to say I do love the south! Along the way we had stopped at all the Welcome Areas as we entered the different states. All were a reflection of the state's pride and individuality. Mississippi's certainly was a beautiful tribute to the old south; an easy relaxed atmosphere and flowers everywhere. However, what caught our eyes was an unusual and simply beautiful carousel horse in the lobby. Kathy picked up a brochure.

We read about a most interesting charity where carousel horses were designed by artists; donations going to a charity for needy children in the Meridian area; then the sponsored horses were put on display at strategic locations around the city. We learned that models of these wonderful artworks could be purchased at Belk-Hudson, again all proceeds going to the charity. We didn't have time to stop as we had Babes and Bevin with us but decided on our return trip we would see if we could find a Belk store. The last fifty miles of this trip went on for an eternity. The road is flat, straight and after driving all night it felt as if I was driving on a treadmill and getting nowhere.

Then there it was Highway 165, we were in Monroe! As we approached the red light where we would turn onto Keystone Road I pointed out the tiny shopping center to Kathy. Like bookends a shop on one corner was "Bandit's", a bar and grill, the other corner was "Gypsy's" a hair salon. "Do you think that is a sign?" I smiled and asked Kathy. She simply said, "Oh my gosh!" We made the turn and I could see the green roofed barn on the left.

Babes and Bevin had been great travelers. They were however happy to step onto ground that wasn't moving. Both settled in nicely and over the next couple of days Kathy and I enjoyed visiting with Carliss and all the horses. We went out to the island and admired what we hoped would be the future home of Belle Rose Farm. However, I wasn't finished in NY so we had to head back, this time without the trailer and horses, so we took our time and tried to have a little rest on the return trip. Of course we did follow our plan to locate a Belk-Hudson store and the lovely carousel horses. We went to the first checkout counter and inquired about the charity. The lady sent us to Customer Service and there they were – hundreds of them; beautiful model horse replicas of these amazing artist's renditions paying tribute to different causes or historical Mississippi events.

Kathy and I knew we each wanted one, but which one, the choice was mindboggling. Then I looked down and saw a well worn book on the bottom shelf of the display. It was an account of the formation of the charity and a description of each horse; its story; and where the original now stood in the city of Meridian.

We learned that actress, Sela Ward, was the charity's founder. I am a big fan. Sela is a fellow alumnus of the University of Alabama which further endears her to me. I have a signed copy of her book and admire her love of family and the south. After looking at all the models I simply could not choose; so I began thumbing through the "Carousel Horses" book and reading the stories hoping this would help me make an appropriate selection – and indeed it did. Suddenly there it was a horse named, "Gypsy". Its story was fascinating. This carousel horse was inspired by the story of Kelly Mitchell, wife of Emil Mitchell, King of the Gypsies of America. It is reported that she died in Coatopa, Alabama while giving birth to her 15th child. She was forty-seven years old. Her body was taken to a funeral home in Meridian, Mississippi and it was determined that the burial site would be in Rose Hill Cemetery. The Gypsy Queen's funeral became a colorful historical event for the city of Meridian and for America's gypsies as well. According to various newspapers and reports of the event at the time approximately 20,000 gypsies made the pilgrimage to pay a final homage to their monarch. Today the grave site remains one of the most visited tourist attractions in Meridian. Visitors often leave gifts on the grave in hopes that Queen Kelly will visit them in a dream and help them with their problems. I have the romantic notion that if Queen Kelly looks down from gypsy heaven she is pleased with the love shown her, but most pleased with the little horse named "Gypsy" in her honor who has given much to children in need. I also know that she probably smiles with pleasure at the beautiful gypsy treasures, Gypsy Vanner Horses, now living not far from her final resting spot.

Back in NY my health worsened; the arthritis was so painful there were days I found it hard to walk. My doctor had changed my meds and this new stuff simply wasn't working. I struggled off to school each day; spent time there cleaning out my office and feeling totally useless. The superintendent did not want either of the retiring administrators to make any preparation for the next year; he wanted the incoming personnel to have complete charge of these tasks. Therefore, work I would normally be doing at this time wasn't there. I sat in my office chair and discovered it had up and down and swivel features I somehow had not had the time to notice before.

A few parents coming in to register their children stopped by to visit; occasionally a staff member came in to check their mail or to say they hadn't quite finished up in their classrooms. It was mindless conversation, just passing time.

In the evening Kathy and I enjoyed quiet fun dinners. I love to cook! ! When I lived in Europe and my daughters were growing up, I'd have dinner parties. The girls and I'd make centerpieces or I'd have the local German flower shop do a lovely one for us. We'd usually set up the table buffet style; all the parties were casual; get your plate and find a seat anywhere you like to visit and have a good time. Those are some of my fondest memories. So, while at Kathy's I cooked. Together we enjoyed the meals, laughed, talked and shared ideas. Kathy is a dear friend, but she is more, she is a colleague, and educator. She makes me think; we loved discussing books we had read, or we would read something at the same time and then discuss our personal take on the subject. Just as we need people in out lives to be our friends, we also need people in our lives who stretch us intellectually, who help us to grow and strive to reach our full potential; for me whether it was in the classroom, kitchen, or now barn, Kathy challenged me to be the best I could be in all those areas. When August came and it was time to go, I knew I'd truly miss this special friend.

The day came; the U-Haul was loaded. Jill and my grandson, Aidan had decided to go south, so they joined me and my three cats. All of us cozily tucked into my truck and away we went. I was most worried about the cats and how they would travel, but they surprised me, sleeping most of the time and when awake if they could see me they were fine. I was determined to make it to Tennessee before stopping; I had made a reservation at a pet friendly motel and we pulled in right around 2 AM. We got a few hours rest and then were off bright and early the next morning.

We almost made it there without incident. Then we came to that long stretch of road through Mississippi and with a loud noise one of the exhaust pipes on my truck disconnected and was dragging on the pavement spitting sparks. I pulled over to the side of the road. Jill got out and assessed the situation. She thought she could tie it up. While she got under to do so I was scared as huge trucks whizzed by without regard enough to at least move over to the far lane. I was much relieved when she returned to the truck and said it might hold. We started out again, but didn't get far before it was dragging once more. Using the GPS we searched for the nearest gas station. There was one just about a mile up the road, so I slowly drove in that direction. Seeing the exit I smiled, the sign announced an Eleanor Roosevelt museum nearby. We pulled into the station where I got out of the truck and kneeled down to see the damage when a rather beat up pick-up truck stopped along side.

The young man got out and asked if I needed help. I said that I sure did. Oh I can help you was his reply. He got some wire from his truck and crawled under asking us how far we had to go while he busily took care of the problem at hand. Pulling himself out from under my truck he said, "That ought to get you where you are going", I thanked him and offered to pay him. "Oh you don't have to do that, Ma'am, it was my pleasure." I watched as his truck rattled away from the station, looking after him to see if a white feather might escape into the air or at least the tip of a wing might be visible. I thought...... I bet Eleanor sent him.

You see, Eleanor Roosevelt, is an idol of mine. On my office bookcase at West Point set a framed photo of Mrs. Roosevelt bearing one of her infamous quotes. I could glance over at it from time to time for inspiration. The quote was, "You must do the thing you think you cannot do." As things worsened on the job or at the farm, or with the increasing pain from my illness this quote became almost my daily mantra.

Before leaving NY I had told Kathy I really wanted to visit Mrs. Roosevelt's cottage in Hyde Park. My daughter, Jamie, and I had visited the Roosevelt home the summer before. During that visit I saw that Mrs. Roosevelt had a desk, a special desk, and I had its twin purchased from an antique shop in Brussels, Belgium. I loved that desk, and now it had a deeper meaning, a connection to a woman I believe could have been my friend had our lives been lived simultaneously. Jamie and I did not have time to make it over to Eleanor's cottage, so now I had Kathy accompany me.

We drove into the parking lot just as a little tram arrived. The driver invited us aboard, but we said we would like to walk. It was a short distance and one I knew Eleanor had made many times. As we approached the gift shop to purchase tickets for the tour, a park ranger encouraged us to hurry on over to the adjoining building where a short video had just begun. The ranger said we could pay for the tickets later. We entered and joined the tour. I loved the cottage; simple, welcoming, it was a place where someone lived; a sleeping porch invited the idea of comfort, cool breezes and enjoying a good book, then drifting off for a brief nap before guests arrived. She was here. This woman who had touched so many lives and left a real legacy for humanity; she was a heroine; she certainly was for me.

As the tour ended Kathy and I wandered a bit over the estate, strolling past the pool, now covered, where FDR swam and across the spacious lawn where the Roosevelt clan held family gatherings. We wound our way back to the gift shop and enjoyed looking over many items celebrating the events in Eleanor's illustrious life. I picked up an autobiography and then a poster I liked. I felt once framed and appropriately hung it would remind me of this special visit. A mother and son who also had arrived late and joined the tour as we had done

Joyce M. Christian

were at the counter. I overheard them as they explained then paid for their items and the tour. Kathy and I placed our things on the counter and when the clerk rang them up we said we needed to pay for the tour as well. Oh you don't have to do that she said with a smile and did not charge us. We thanked her and walked out. I turned to Kathy who just smiled; I said, "You know Eleanor just gave us a tour of her home." "I know," said Kathy.

Now, as Jill and I left the gas station with the exhaust pipe secured by an unknown man I chose to recognize as an Eleanor angel, I could not help but smile and breathe a sigh of gratitude. About an hour later I made the left hand turn onto Keystone Road and saw the green roofed barn at Carliss' I was more than relieved; I was home. Now retired and in Louisiana I was at the beginning of this final chapter in my life.....I was excited, hopeful, and yes, anxious. Initially the plan had been for the new place to be well underway by my arrival; bankers and land deals had slowed the process. Carliss had had some difficulty selling the front half of her property and this was needed to make the necessary down payment for the new mortgage loan. For the time being the humans all crowded into a too small house; and fourteen horses were side by side in a too small barn with one paddock. We tried our best to keep our spirits up, but as time passed and we didn't seem to be getting beyond deadlock; frustration rose and tempers flared. I believe the only thing that kept us going was our joint belief in this horse farm; a farm that both Carliss and I had dreamed of having; both as little girls had wanted, and now if we could just hold on to the dream and the friendship it could be ours – it could be our reality.

Jill and Aidan had gone on to stay with a friend in Texas and I had sought out a young rider/trainer to help primarily with my stallions. Her name was Bridgette Summerville. Cushti Bok's Lord Marlborough, my Lordi, had been a testosterone handful for inexperienced Carliss. Now that I was back and I had Bridgette's help he was calming down and starting to be manageable once again. The horses had all adapted to their current situation; they knew their routine, when it was time to eat, be turned out, worked or groomed. They tolerated with unbelievable patience the human forced schedule they lived. Carliss and I longed for the new place, where we could have adequate paddock space and an arena for working and training. While Carliss loved the caring and tending to of the horses, I loved to see them worked under saddle or driving. I no longer rode, but I loved to drive and was anxious to get Bandit going again. Carliss' Piper also had been trained to drive and I was looking forward to driving him. I also in the last couple of months in NY with Babes and Bevin had grown fond of doing ground work. I had even begun a little at liberty work with Babes and while I am no trainer or professional, I loved that my horse respected me and seemed to know I wanted to dance with him. I ached to get to a place where I could take all this up again.

From August until October we waited. The dates for closing changed constantly. We couldn't plan on anything. Finances were tight; costs were increasing and Carliss, Jerry and I began to wonder if we were making the right decision.

"With faith, love, and this unlikely gift you may find yourself someplace you've never imagined."

- from the movie, Mr. Magorium's Wonder Emporium

*J*n October I drove to Ohio for the second Gypsy Vanner Horse Society Breed Seminar and first GV Horse Evaluation. Again, Wayne Hipsley exceeded our expectations with a wonderful educational seminar, followed by hands on with live horses enabling students to visually grasp the quality expectation in the Vanner Horse.

A small number of horses attended the evaluation, but it was a beginning. Those who came to see just what this involved and whether it was worthwhile experienced total professionalism. All who attended left realizing the importance this step held for the preservation and promotion of the breed.

Driving back through Tennessee and over long, lonely rural Louisiana roads gave me time to reflect. I was happy. The GVHS had been through so much; when this organization was under attack, the breed was under attack; the battles had been tough, but this first GV Horse Evaluation took root in my brain; I saw those magnificent stallions standing quietly while Wayne poked and prodded to find that rib or that shoulder; proudly waiting and taking direction from the handler, thick mane and tail carefully groomed most often met the feather blanketing their ample hooves. This breed was incredible, they were horses like no other – I loved them. In this last chapter of my life I simply wanted to do what I could to help the world not lose this gift.

Yes, I said gift. While I know there are horse lovers out there who would argue that all horses are gifts – I see a greater gift in the Vanner Horse. I loved a Quarter Horse named Sugarfoot who shared a brief moment in my life – he gave me experiences that I certainly remember and hold to, but my Vanners have given me so much more. They know me. They desire to know me, and more than that they want to please me. Even when Bandit is being Mr. Grumpy and he can be, he still prefers this old gray haired lady and comes when I call or stops when I twill my voice as he was taught to do during his driving training. He still falls asleep on the crossties as I brush him and brush away my cares, opening sleepy eyes just to check if it is still me controlling the brush.

Carliss is a stroke survivor; she knew nothing about horses; just was encouraged to get into equine therapy to help with her balance. Her five Vanners saved her and gave her life back; it is amazing to watch her direct them with her voice alone. They know; they take care of her; she asks them to wait and to not let her fall – and they do it! !

From December until January we anticipated the new place ready for our move – yet delays continued; costs rose; stress grew. I begged Jill to return to help with the horses. We had stallions, mares, and geldings all crowded in this too small barn. I needed Jill to help Bridgett, the young trainer. At the end of February I left Carliss in the good, capable hands of these two young horsewomen while I flew to Florida to attend the GVHS Annual Meeting and third Breed Standard Seminar and second GV Horse Evaluation. This was an exciting event; it was a measuring stick to see how well the organization was progressing with this new program.

Thanks to the Board of Directors (Bill Ricci, Bob Smith, Mike Litz, Sue Rathbone, and myself), along with Barb Snyder, our Registrar/Treasurer the three day event held at the Florida Carriage Museum and Resort was a monumental success. We had wonderful attendance including respected, well known equine judges seeking to obtain their GVHS Judge's Card. Our members came from all over to include:

California, Canada, Colorado, Ohio, Pennsylvania, the Carolinas, Georgia, Minnesota, Louisiana, Texas, and Florida. The Annual Meeting highlights included the awarding of the first newly designed belt buckle award to Dennis Thompson. The inscription read, "The Dream Maker". It was presented to Mr. Thompson by GVHS Youth Member, Ariel Folk, whose idea it was to use belt buckles as awards.

She took this on as a project and earned the money to have the buckle mold made – it was also her idea to have the first one go to Mr. Thompson. This was a special moment in time as I looked at Ariel handing the award to Dennis – the co-founder being recognized most appropriately by the future of the GVHS and this breed – you could feel the emotion in the room; the right kind of emotion – gratitude, celebration, and joy.

To lighten things up a bit an auction was held to raise much needed operating funds for the GVHS. Robert Folk and Mike Litz as auctioneers really got into their role and members opened their wallets, got out their check books, bought treasures to take home and the GVHS bank account rose by over $13,000!

I returned home to Louisiana and focused my attention on Belle Rose Farm. Finally the house was going up and the barn had gotten underway. Over the next few weeks that followed we watched the new farm take form. We also were eagerly awaiting the first foal of this joint adventure – Carliss' mare, Ambrosia was in foal to my stallion, Babes. We wanted the horses all moved over to the new barn before the foal's birth. A spacious mare stall was ready and waiting there. The night before the move we checked Ambrosia, though early signs of foaling were there, it appeared still a few days away. The following morning Carliss and I entered the barn to feed and I went over to get hay. Suddenly I realized Ambrosia, who loves her food and usually greets us with mumblings and mouth pressed against the bars, was standing quietly in the middle of her stall not moving. Memories of Magic following the birth of her foals came flashing through my head and smiling I walked quietly over to peer into the stall. Standing proudly nursing was our new born colt. The placenta had passed and lay in a mucky pile on the stall floor. I turned to Carliss and said, "Carliss, we have a new baby."

At first she thought I was kidding and then grabbed me and gave me a hug when she saw the foal. He was black and white; his markings were almost identical on each side. His head was black with a white splash at the top and a little white snip like his sire. A black tail was an added plus. He was strong and healthy, alert, and full of life. Standing in front of us was the beginning of Belle Rose Farm.

Belle Rose Rajah with dam, Ambrosia

We moved to the new facility an eighteen stall "H" style barn with an attached covered, open air, arena. Ambrosia and the foal made the twenty minute trip without any trouble and seemed quite pleased with their spacious new abode. Carliss' nieces came to see the baby. We had been trying to find just the right name for him and then her niece said, "What about Rajah?" He did act like a little king; we felt the name suited him and so he was officially named Belle Rose Rajah. We were so grateful Ambrosia was fine, that the foal was here; safe and sound – the first of what we hoped would be more to come.

Things don't always turn out like you plan; yet, the hope that this farm would become the fulfillment of our dreams continued to be strong. Through the tough first six months of being in Louisiana, Carliss and I had come to realize we do have differences. We had come a long way by respecting those for the sake of our farm. Originally I was to co-own the farm; this agreement was an important part of my decision to come to Louisiana – the chance to once again own my own place. Carliss wanted a big house; I just wanted the necessities of comfort met – place to eat, sleep, and relax with a good book or watch an old movie (can't handle current reality TV) – a personal space for my cats and me, with my treasured horses nearby. Carliss and Jerry have the house; I stayed for a while with them, but it was not right. My things remained boxed waiting for "home" wherever that was going to be. Given everything I went through during my time in NY; the opportunity to be at home; to have a real home without worry of ever having to be faced with relocating again remains an important part of my dream.

After all my moves my belongings have dwindled down to only those things that hold personal value – fond reminders of favorite life moments. For now those books, mementos, pictures, and knick knacks acquired through years of traveling and experiencing the world (maybe I am a Gypsy) are at present tucked away in boxes waiting for that right place.

However, I did pull out two things that are ever present reminders of keeping the faith as well as just how far my journey has taken me. These special items provide a daily hint that giving up on any part of my dream can never be an option. One is a plaque with Jeremiah 29:11 on it. The other is a framed print of Lynn Wade's painting, "Magic In the Air", of Cushti Bok playing on a hillside above a gypsy camp. It was graciously given to me by Lynn and Dennis Thompson following the 2008 GVHS Annual Meeting.

I am amazed at the life I have been allowed to live; my dream is well on its way to being fulfilled; and who knows what other plans for hope and prosperity God has in store. He certainly has been more than gracious thus far. His promise, and the years of watching its truth unfold for me, brings to mind the words of a favorite hymn, "To God be the glory, great things He hath done." And I might add I believe He will do.

The teacher in me sees just how much I have learned along the way and sees much more learning ahead. My personal work has taught me just how important learning is – it should be recognized as a life-long pursuit. It is my hope that with the horses I can help rekindle that way of thinking through youth programs – 4-H; Agriculture in the Classroom; and others. Horses are great teachers for showing you that you don't know everything you thought you did. This is such a valuable lesson for our young people today. To be involved with the development of these programs would simply multiply the rewards of my life's travels.

I borrow a quote taken from yet another favorite book, *"A Whole New Mind"* by Daniel H. Pink – "......adding the capacity for art and heart to our penchant of logic and analysis, won't be easy. Few worthwhile things ever are. But maybe that's the point. As Victor Frankl could have told us, the ideal life is not a fear-fueled pursuit of cheese. It's more like walking a labyrinth, where the purpose is the journey itself."

My journey took me to Belle Rose Farm. A new welcome to Sterlington sign was put up just a few days before we moved to the new farm. It reads:

"Welcome to Sterlington – Faith, Family and Friends."

Sign, fate, both or neither those are the ingredients that brought me here. It also begs me to share another Eleanor quote. At Hyde Park in December 1960 she scribed the following taken from the preface of her autobiography:

"We all of us owe, I imagine, far more than we realize to our friends as well as to the members of our family. I know that in my own case my friends are responsible for much that I have become and without them there are many things which would have remained closed books to me." I simply echo Eleanor's thoughts as without my friends and my family I would not have reached this point in my journey.

My horses are gifts to me; they are my passion; I believe they are unique and have great potential for serving mankind; they certainly have the ability to tap into an untouched group of horse lovers (Baby Boomers who always wanted horses). Vanner intelligence and manageability make them not only suitable, but ideal for equine therapy and equine assisted education programs. As a teacher I see where this combination would be highly successful both for breed and people.

I hope as more and more individuals come to understand this breed and the potential these horses have for good they too will share their stories. We live in a world which has removed itself from nature and its natural rhythm. Horses encourage a return to a slower pace, a daily life pattern grounded in a simpler more peaceful style; these are important lessons and today's children need to be aware of such choices. Horses invite relationship; one founded in daily interaction and communication. Over time such a relationship can and does build mutual understanding and respect. Within an equine environment many more life skills become apparent and are learned in partnership with the horses. While I know of many programs using a variety of breeds to meet this ever growing need, it is my personal belief that the Vanner Horse could be an exceptional star in this arena.

As I have shared my journey with these wonderful horses I recalled situations and circumstances that have been stumbling blocks for the recognition and appreciation of the Gypsy Vanner breed. While there is a movement to simply lump all horses from gypsies into one category, Gypsy Horses, this would in my opinion not be in the best interest of the truly unique and rare animal that Cindy Thompson and Fred Walker named

Gypsy Vanner Horse. I dare say it could be that the true Gypsy Vanner Horse is rarer today than it was in 1996. Due to mass importation of any and all horses from gypsies; due to expanded cross breeding to get size differences and odd colors to meet the demands of an American market gone wild; and of course due to gypsies continuing to breed the way they always have. On the other hand I do believe there are a few true lovers of the Gypsy Vanner Horse. Owners and breeders who have not been swayed by all of this, rather they have been totally captivated by the Vanners that are in their lives. This group of Vanner Horse enthusiasts understands the "magic" in this breed; they want to protect, preserve and without a doubt share it with those who can understand it and appreciate the important differences in these horses. It is my hope that through the educational seminars and breed evaluations begun by the Gypsy Vanner Horse Society the Vanner Horse will surface as the truly special equine it is.

I had hoped that Belle Rose Farm would be home and a shared adventure, but time revealed it simply could not be. Carliss and I are much too different. So, as I began to close this work my horses, cats and me were once again true gypsies – traveling souls in search of that elusive dream – "home". In August, I had begun a part time job at a really unique school. Remarkably, their theme for the school year was, "Dare to Dream". When I went for my job interview with the Director, she shared they had been hoping someone with horses would come along. One of the teachers was a horse person and wanted to work with me on a new equine assisted education program – we began with five of her students. That program has begun for us a new adventure – an incredible new facility – new friends and a bigger dream than I could have ever imagined. God is good – He keeps his promises. This is the beginning of another chapter in my life; one that appears to be much blessed and prosperous. I am grateful and will keep a daily journal as this dream unfolds to be shared in possibly another book.

In the meantime my goal will continue to be to share the unique and wonderful abilities of this rare horse in order to do some good, to heal some pain, to share a bit of joy along the way. I wish for all my readers to find strength, faith, courage, and the persistence and determination required to follow your dreams – they can and do come true. I send you off with my best wishes for wonderful life travels – a traveling wish from my childhood memories – Dale Evans and Roy Rogers sent their viewers off with the phrase – Happy trails to you....and now today I close with the name of one of my favorite Gypsy Vanner Horse stallions, *Latcho Drom*. Latcho is owned by Dennis Thompson and his name means – safe journey.

Joyce and her beloved Gypsy Vanner stallion, Babes
Photographed by Vanessa Wright Capone for The Literary Horse

The Vanner's Secret
By Joyce M. Christian

What is this horse?
From whence did it come?
Black and white, yet not like other horses,
Not even some.
What is this feeling...?
This incredible sense of contentment;
Peace, and yes this hint of hope?
What is it? Does it come from this creature?
Yes it does!
Its beauty draws you near, its invitation to play,
Makes you stay;
No fear; just trust
Felt and understood,
Somehow, some way.
Intelligence so great you expect it to speak,
With voice quiet, its soft eyes convey every message.
Your hands or face sink deep into its winter coat,
And you disappear into your own world;
All worries and troubles are far away and gone.
The only explanation for such magic...
They must indeed be Unicorns!

Cushti Bok
(Photo courtesy of Mary Beth Wherry)

163

Breinigsville, PA USA
15 February 2011
255645BV00001B/14/P